# ALLSENSORS 2021

The Sixth International Conference on Advances in Sensors, Actuators, Metering and Sensing

July 18 – 22, 2021

Nice, France

**ALLSENSORS 2021 Editors**

Paulo E. Cruvinel, Embrapa Instrumentation, Brazil
Manuel Vieira. CTS-UNINOVA, Portugal

**Printed from e-media with permission by:**

Curran Associates, Inc.
57 Morehouse Lane
Red Hook, NY 12571

**Some format issues inherent in the e-media version may also appear in this print version.**



Printed with permission by Curran Associates, Inc. (2023)

International Academy, Research, and Industry Association (IARIA)
412 Derby Way
Wilmington, DE 19810

Phone: (408) 893-6407
Fax: (408) 527-6351

petre@iaria.org

**Additional copies of this publication are available from:**

Curran Associates, Inc.
57 Morehouse Lane
Red Hook, NY 12571 USA
Phone: 845-758-0400
Fax: 845-758-2633
Email: curran@proceedings.com
Web: www.proceedings.com

**Table of Contents**

# ALLSENSORS 2021

# Forward

The Sixth International Conference on Advances in Sensors, Actuators, Metering and Sensing (ALLSENSORS 2021), held in Nice, France, July 18 - 22, 2021, covered related topics on theory practice and applications of sensor devices, techniques, data acquisition and processing, and on wired and wireless sensors and sensor networks.

Sensor networks and sensor-based systems support many applications today above ground. Underwater operations and applications are quite limited by comparison. Most applications refer to remotely controlled submersibles and wide-area data collection systems at a coarse granularity. Other remote sensing domains and applications are using special sensing devices and services. Transducers and actuators complement the monitoring and control and constitute an area of interest related to sensors. They make use of specific sensor-based measurements and convey appropriate control actions.

ALLSENSORS 2021 was intended to serve as a forum for researchers from the academia and the industry, professionals, standard developers, policy makers, investors and practitioners to present their recent results, to exchange ideas, and to establish new partnerships and collaborations.

The accepted papers covered a large spectrum of topics on techniques and applications, best practices, awareness and experiences as well as future trends and needs (both in research and practice) related to all aspects of sensor-based applications and services.

We take here the opportunity to warmly thank all the members of the ALLSENSORS 2021 technical program committee as well as the numerous reviewers. The creation of such a broad and high quality conference program would not have been possible without their involvement. We also kindly thank all the authors that dedicated much of their time and efforts to contribute to the ALLSENSORS 2021. We truly believe that thanks to all these efforts, the final conference program consists of top quality contributions.

This event could also not have been a reality without the support of many individuals, organizations and sponsors. In addition, we also gratefully thank the members of the ALLSENSORS 2021 organizing committee for their help in handling the logistics and for their work that is making this professional meeting a success.

We hope the ALLSENSORS 2021 was a successful international forum for the exchange of ideas and results between academia and industry and to promote further progress on the topics of sensors.

**ALLSENSORS 2021 Chairs**

**ALLSENSORS Steering Committee**

Michael Niedermayer, Beuth University of Applied Sciences - Berlin, Germany
Paulo E. Cruvinel, Embrapa Instrumentation, Brazil
Matteo Tonezzer, CNR-IMEM, Trento, Italy
Almudena Rivadeneyra, Universidad de Granada, Spain
Sandrine Bernardini, Aix Marseille University, France

**ALLSENSORS 2021 Advisory Committee**

Manuel Vieira, CTS-ISEL, Portugal
Manuela Vieira, ISEL-ADEETC ; CTS-UNINOVA; DEE-FCT-UNL, Portugal

**ALLSENSORS 2021 Publicity Chair**

Alvaro Liebana, Universitat Politecnica de Valencia, Spain
Mar Parra, Universitat Politecnica de Valencia, Spain

# ALLSENSORS 2021

# COMMITTEE

**ALLSENSORS Steering Committee**
Michael Niedermayer, Beuth University of Applied Sciences - Berlin, Germany
Paulo E. Cruvinel, Embrapa Instrumentation, Brazil
Matteo Tonezzer, CNR-IMEM, Trento, Italy
Almudena Rivadeneyra, Universidad de Granada, Spain
Sandrine Bernardini, Aix Marseille University, France

**ALLSENSORS 2021 Advisory Committee**

Manuel Vieira, CTS-ISEL, Portugal
Manuela Vieira, ISEL-ADEETC ; CTS-UNINOVA; DEE-FCT-UNL, Portugal

**ALLSENSORS 2021 Publicity Chair**

Alvaro Liebana, Universitat Politecnica de Valencia, Spain
Mar Parra, Universitat Politecnica de Valencia, Spain

**ALLSENSORS 2021 Technical Program Committee**

Francesco Aggogeri, University of Brescia, Italy
Amin Al-Habaibeh, Nottingham Trent University, UK
Ammar Al-Jodah, Monash University, Australia
Youssef N. Altherwy, Imperial College London, UK
Kawiwat Amnatchotiphan, Rangsit University, Thailand
Darius Andriukaitis, Kaunas University of Technology, Lithuania
Farzad Asgarian, University of Michigan, Ann Arbor, USA
Herve Aubert, Laboratory for Analysis and Architecture of Systems (LAAS-CNRS), France
Roberto Beghi, Università degli Studi di Milano, Italy
Fateh Benmahmoud, Grenoble-INP. - Université Grenoble-Alpes, France
Roc Berenguer Pérez, TECNUN - Technological Campus of the University of Navarra, Spain
Sandrine Bernardini, Aix Marseille University, France
Xavier Boddaert, Mines Saint Etienne | Centre Microélectronique de Provence (CMP), France
Ismail Butun, Chalmers University of Technology, Sweden
Maria Candelaria Hernandez Goya, Universidad de La Laguna, Spain
Juan Vicente Capella Hernández, Universitat Politècnica de València, Spain
Vítor Carvalho, 2AI-EST-IPCA / Algoritmi Research Centre - UM, Portugal
Paula María Castro Castro, Universidade da Coruña, Spain
Debashish Chakravarty, IIT Khaargpur, India
Nan-Fu Chiu, National Taiwan Normal University,Taiwan
Paulo E. Cruvinel, Embrapa Instrumentation, Brazil
Francesco G. Della Corte, University of Napoli "Federico II", Italy
Emiliano Descrovi, Polytechnic University of Turin, Italy
Chérif Diallo, Université Gaston Berger (UGB), Senegal

**Copyright Information**

# Wayfinding Services in Crowded Buildings Through Visible Light

Manuela Vieira, Manuel Augusto Vieira, Paula Louro, Alessandro Fantoni
ADETC/ISEL/IPL,
R. Conselheiro Emídio Navarro, 1959-007
Lisboa, Portugal
CTS-UNINOVA
Quinta da Torre, Monte da Caparica, 2829-516,
Caparica, Portugal

e-mail: mv@isel.ipl.pt, mv@isel.pt, plouro@deetc.isel.pt, afantoni@deetc.isel.ipl.pt

Pedro Vieira
ADETC/ISEL/IPL,
R. Conselheiro Emídio Navarro, 1959-007
Lisboa, Portugal
Instituto das Telecomunicações
Instituto Superior Técnico, 1049-001,
Lisboa, Portugal
e-mail: pvieira@isel.pt

*Abstract*— **This paper investigates the applicability of an intuitive risk of transmission wayfinding system in public spaces, virtual races, indoor large environments and complex buildings using Visible Light Communication (VLC). Typical scenarios include: finding places, like a particular shop or office, guiding users across different floors, and through elevators and stairs. The system is able to inform the users, in real time, not only of the best route to the desired destination, through a route without clusters of users, but also of crowded places. Data from the sender is encoded, modulated and converted into light signals emitted by the transmitters. Tetra-chromatic white sources are used providing a different data channel for each chip. At the receiver side, the modulated light signal, containing the ID and the 3D geographical position of the transmitter and wayfinding information, is received by a SiC optical sensor with light filtering and demultiplexing properties. Since lighting and wireless data communication is combined, each luminaire for downlink transmission becomes a single cell, in which the optical Access Point (AP) is located in the ceiling and the mobile users are scattered across the overlap discs of each cell, underneath. The light signals emitted by the LEDs are interpreted directly by the receivers of the positioned users. Bidirectional communication is tested. The effect of the location of the Aps is evaluated and a 3D model for the cellular network is analyzed. In order to convert the floorplan to a 3D geometry, a tandem of layers in a orthogonal topology is used, and a 3D localization design, demonstrated by a prototype implementation, is presented. Uplink transmission is implemented, and the 3D best route to navigate through venue is calculated. Buddy wayfinding services are also considered. The results showed that the dynamic VLC navigation system enables to determine the position of a mobile target inside the network, to infer the travel direction along the time, to interact with received information and to optimize the route towards a static or dynamic destination.**

***Keywords-*** *Visible Light Communication; Indoor navigation; Bidirectional Communication; Wayfinding; Optical sensors;Multiplexing/demultiplexing techniques.*

## I. INTRODUCTION

Optical wireless communication has been widely studied during the last years in short-range applications. Therefore, communications within personal working/living spaces are highly demanded. The availability of portable communication devices, such as smartphones and tablets increases the demand on mobile wireless connectivity. Several technologies have been investigated to provide wireless connections to the users in indoor and outdoor environments. Nowadays, indoor positioning methods are mainly based on Wi-Fi, Bluetooth, Radio-Frequency Identification (RFID) and Visible Light Communications (VLC) [1][2][3][4]. VLC is a data transmission technology [5] that can easily be employed in indoor environments since it can use the existing LED lighting infrastructure with simple modifications [6][7]. VLC can be regarded as a light based Wi-Fi, i.e., instead of radio waves uses visible light to transmit the data. It presents advantages when compared with the Wi-Fi, namely the invulnerability to the hackers since it does not penetrate through the wall, its high capacity and efficiency. Once lights are essential part of operating rooms, the VLC technology finds applications in a wide variety of fields like: in medical and healthcare, in airlines and aviation, in supermarkets and railway stations, in retail stores, in hidden communication or in Line-of -Sight (LoS) applications as in traffic control, vehicle to vehicle communication or smart street lighting.

The VLC systems use the wavelength range between 380 nm and 780 nm and the LEDs are used as light sources and transmitters. Therefore, the LEDs are twofold by providing illumination, as well as communication. LEDs are incoherent light sources and transmitting information can only be realized by the optical intensity change. Here, the On-OFF keying (OOK) modulation scheme is used. In the sequence, we propose to use modulated visible light, carried out by white tetra-chromatic low cost LEDs. The use of those LEDs provides different data channel for each chip offering the possibility of Wavelength Division Multiplexing (WDM), which enhances the transmission data rate. At the receiver side, the modulated light signal is received by a SiC photodetector, based on a tandem a-SiC:H/a-Si:H pin/pin structure, that presents light filtering and demultiplexing properties decoding the received information[8 [9]. Here, when different visible signals are encoded in the same optical transmission path, the device multiplexes the different optical channels, performs different filtering processes (amplification, switching, and wavelength conversion) and finally decodes the encoded signals recovering the transmitted information.

Research is still necessary to design LED arrangements that can optimize communication performance while meeting the illumination constraints for a variety of large indoor layouts. Visible light can be used as an ID system in different places such as buildings and subways and can be employed for identifying the room number and its building. The main idea is to divide the space into spatial beams originating from the different ID light sources, and identify each beam with a unique timed sequence of light signals. Fine-grained indoor localization can enable several applications; in airports, supermarkets and shopping malls. Exact location of products can greatly improve the customer's shopping experience and enable customer analytics and marketing [10]. The signboards, based on arrays of LEDs, positioned in strategic directions to broadcast the information [11], are modulated acting as down- and up-link channels in the bidirectional communication.

In this paper, a LED-supported positioning and navigation VLC system is proposed. After the Introduction, in Section II, a VLC scenario for large environments is established, the emitters and receivers are characterized and the communication protocol presented. In Section III, the main experimental results are presented, the effect of the location of the optical Access Points (Aps) is evaluated and a model for the different cellular networks is analysed. Square and hexagon mesh are tested, and a 2D localization design, demonstrated by a prototype implementation, is presented. Uplink transmission is implemented and the 2D best route to navigate through venue calculated. In section IV the conclusions are drawn showing that the system make possible to determine the position of a mobile target inside the network, to infer the travel direction along the time and to interact with information received.

## II. VLC NETWORK

In the follow the VLC network is described.

### A. *Architecture*

The scenario simulated is an airport. Here, the raveler, equipped with a receiver, navigates from outdoor to indoor. It sends a request message to find the right track and, in the available time, he adds customized points of interest and halls to boarding. During his path, the passenger is advised how to reach its destination and the possibility to use location based advertising services. The requested information is sent by the emitters at the ceiling to its receiver. In Figure 1, the proposed architecture and scenario are illustrated.

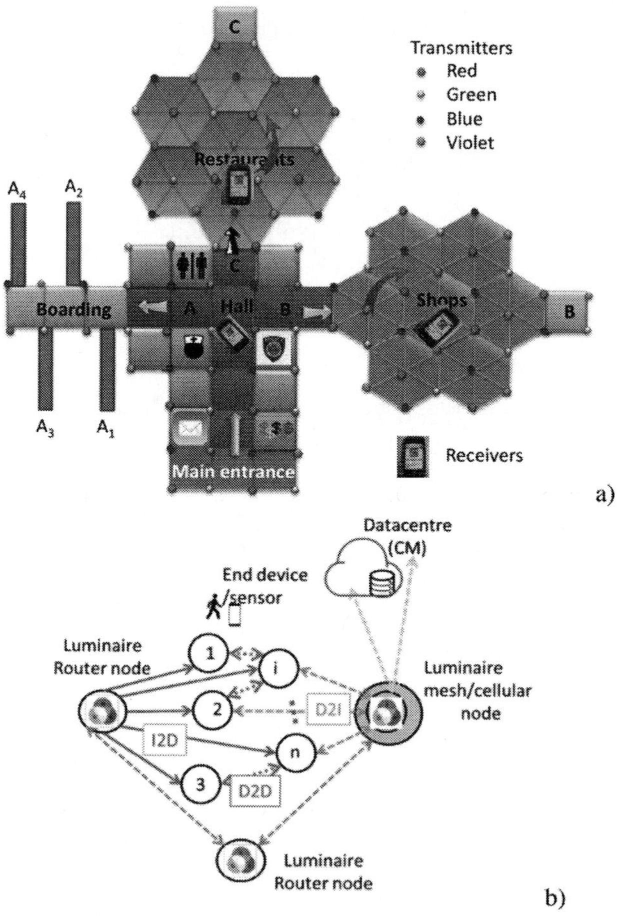


Figure 1 a) Optical infrastructure and indoor layout.b) a) Mesh and cellular hybrid architecture

Two topologies were considered: the square for the main hall and the hexagonal for the marketing zones (Figure 1a). Data from the infrastructure is encoded, modulated and converted into light signals emitted by the transmitters. Tetra-chromatic (Red, Green, Blue, Violet) white sources are used, providing a different data channel for each chip. At the receiver side, the modulated light signal, containing the ID and the 2D geographical position of the transmitter and wayfinding information, is received by a SiC photodetector with light filtering and demultiplexing properties. To synchronize the signals from multiple LEDs, the transmitters use different IDs, allowing the signal to be reconstructed at the receiver.

Although not the scope of this paper, we propose a mesh cellular hybrid structure to create a gateway-less system without any external gateways needed. We propose this network configuration since it is wireless and ad-hoc. It spans all devices, is wire free, demonstrate resiliency to physical obstructions and adapt to changes in the transmission medium. Therefore, a mesh network is a good fit because it dynamically reconfigures itself and grows to the size of any installation. Is also a secure and trustworthy network [12]. As illustrated in Figure 1b, the luminaires, in this architecture, are equipped with one of two types of nodes: A "mesh" controller that connects with other nodes in its vicinity. These controllers can forward messages to other devices (I2D) in the mesh, effectively acting like routers nodes in the network. A "mesh/cellular" hybrid controller, that is also equipped with a modem providing IP base connectivity to the central manager services (CM). These nodes acts as border-router and can be used for edge computing. Under this architecture, the short-range mesh network purpose is twofold: enable edge computing and device-to-cloud communication, by ensuring a secure communication from a luminaire controller to the edge computer or datacenter (I2CM), through a neighbor luminaire controller with an active cellular connection; and enable peer-to-peer communication ($I2I_{IP}$), to exchange information between smart devices.

### *B. Large Environments emitters and receivers*

The principal components of the VLC system are the LEDs, which acts as the communication sources and the SiC WDM devices that serves as receiving element. Data from the sender is converted into an intermediate data representation, byte format, and converted into light signals emitted by the transmitter module. The light signal is received by the WDM photodetector that detects the on/off states of the LEDs, generates a binary sequence of the received signals and convert data into the original format.

The LEDs emit light when the energy levels change in the semiconductor diode. The wavelength depends on the semiconductor material used to form the LED chip. For data transmission, commercially available polychromatic white LEDs were used at the nodes of the network. On each node only one chip is modulated for data transmission and carries useful information while the others are only supplied with DC to maintain white colour illumination. Red (R; 626 nm), Green (G;530 nm), Blue (B; 470 nm) and violet (V; 390 nm) LEDs, are used [13][14]. Since lighting and wireless data communication is combined, each luminaire for downlink transmission become a single cell, in which the optical access point (AP) is located in the ceiling and the mobile users are scattered within the overlap discs of each cells underneath.

Lighting in large environments is designed to illuminate the entire space in a uniform way. Ceiling plans for the LED array layout is shown in Figure 2. Two topologies considered: the square, (Figure 2a) and the hexagonal (Figure 2b). In the square lattice topology the cells have squares shapes while in the hexagonal one they are distributed to form a hexagonal shaped constellation. To receive the information from several transmitters, the receiver must be positioned where the circles from each transmitter overlaps, producing at the receiver, a multiplexed (MUX) signal that, after demultiplexing, acts twofold as a positioning system and a data transmitter.

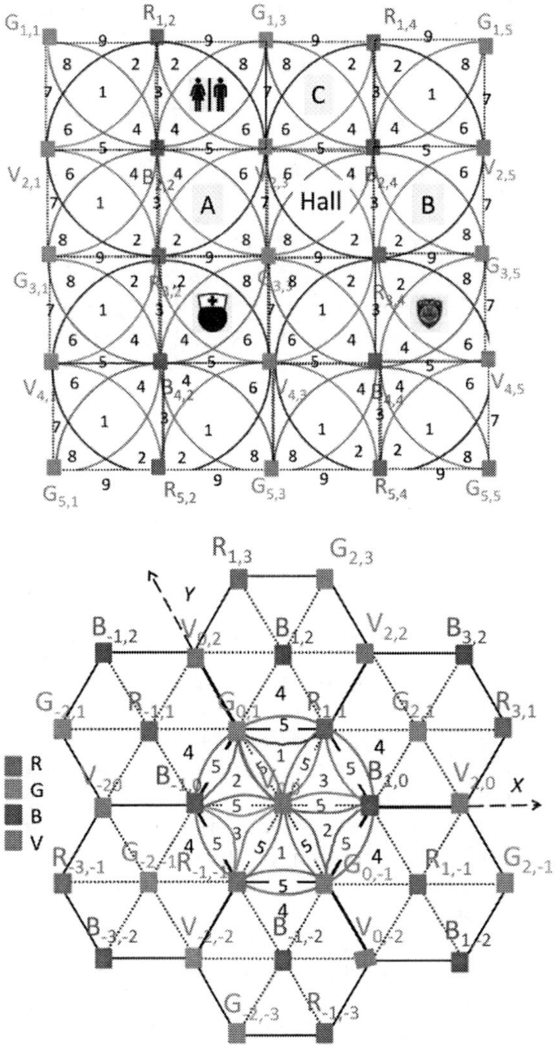


Figure 2. Illustration of the optical scenarios (RGBV >modulated LEDs spots). Cellular topologies: a) Clusters of cells in square topology . b) Clusters of cell in hexagonal topology.

In both topologies, each node, $X_{I,j}$, carries its own color, X, (RGBV) as well as its ID position in the network (I,j). In both, the grid sizes were chosen to avoid overlap in the receiver from adjacent grid points. The overlap regions (footprints) are pointed out in Figure 2 and reported in Table 1. The device receives multiple signals, finds the centroid of the received coordinates and stores it as the reference point position. Users in different locations are served simultaneously by the same transmitter leading to a fine grained implementation. Due to the overlapping coverage area of adjacent Aps joint transmission exists. In Table I, and for both topologies, the overlap regions below each AP (footprints) are displayed.

TABLE 1 FINE-GRAINED TOPOLOGIES: FOOTPRINT REGIONS.

| Footprint regions | Square topology | Hexagonal topology |
|---|---|---|
| #1 | RGBV | RGV |
| #2 | RGB | GBV |
| #3 | RB | RBV |
| #4 | RBV | RGB |
| #5 | BV | RGBV |
| #6 | GBV | - |
| #7 | GV | - |
| #8 | RGV | - |
| #9 | RG | - |

The VLC photosensitive receiver is a two terminal double PIN photodetector based on a multilayer heterostructure, p-I'(a-SiC:H)-n/p-i(a-Si:H)-n. Two transparent front and back contacts are used [8]. The device presents high sensitivity and linear response in the visible range generating at the terminals a proportional photocurrent. It fast response enables the possibility of high speed communications. Modulated light supplied by the polychromatic LEDs is used for data transmission. The signals are encoded into colours intensities emitted by red, green, blue and violet LEDs. The generated photocurrent is processed using a transimpedance circuit and the proportional voltage is processed, by using signal conditioning techniques (adaptive bandpass filtering and amplification, triggering and demultiplexing), until the data signal is reconstructed at the data processing unit (digital conversion, decoding and decision) [13].

### C. *Modulation technique*

An on-off keying (OOK) modulation scheme was used providing a good trade-off between system performance and implementation complexity. The OOK transmits data by sequentially turning *on* and *off* the LED providing digital dimming support. To create a communication protocol to ensure the required system performance and overcome the technology constraints, a 32 bits data frame was designed. Three control fields, one for synchronism (Sync.) and two for the identification of the cell (ID) begin each frame. This sequence is followed by a fourth block that is for the payload, as it is shown, for both topologies, in Figure 3. A stop bit is used at the end of each frame.

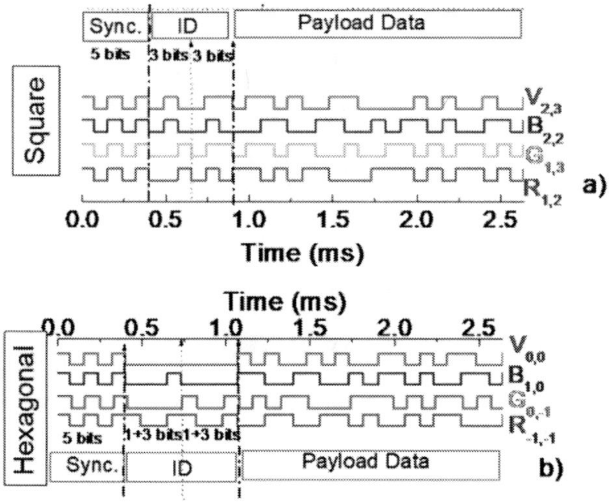


Figure 3. Data frame structure. Representation one encoded message, in a time slot from the array in the network: a) Square topology; $R_{12}$ ; $G_{1,3}$ ; $B_{2,2}$ and $V_{2,3}$ are the transmitted node packet. B) Hexagonal topology; $R_{-1,-1}$; $G_{0,-1}$; $B_{1,0}$ and $V_{0,0}$ are the transmitted node packet.

The first five bits in the frame are used for time synchronization. The same synchronization header [10101], in an ON-OFF pattern, is imposed simultaneously to all emitters. Each colour signal (RGBV) carries its own ID-BIT, so, the next bits give the coordinates of the emitter inside the array ($X_{i,j}$). Cell's IDs are encoded using a binary representation for the decimal number. In the square topology (Figure 3a) six bits are used: the first three for the binary code of the line and the other three for the column. In the hexagonal topology, 60º Cartesian coordinates were applied (Figure 2b). Here, An extra bit was added at the beginning of the binary code to represent the number's sign: setting that bit to *0* is for a positive number, and setting it to *1* is for a negative number. The remaining bits in the number indicate the absolute value. So, the next eight bits (ID) are assigned, respectively, to the *x* and *y* coordinate (*I,j*) of the emitter in the array (Figure 3b). For both, the last bits, in the frame, are reserved for the message send by the $X_{ij}$ node (payload data). With this information, the method will give an unique answer, *i.e.*, the location of the receiver in the array ($X_{i,j}$) and the broadcast information.

Results show that in the square network $R_{1,2}$ , $G_{1,3,}$ $B_{2,2}$ and $V_{2,3}$ are the transmitted node packets, in a time slot, from the unit cell where the restrooms are located (Figure 2a). In the hexagonal network, the nodes $R_{-1,-1,}$ $G_{0,-1,}$ $B_{1,0}$ and $V_{0,0}$, at the first ring of the restaurant zone (Figure 2b) are the transmitters.

## III. EXPERIMENTAL RESULTS AND DISCUSSION

Main results are discussed.

### *A. Decoding, Positioning and point-to-point Route*

In a data frame, the MUX signal at the receiver, due to the joint transmission of four R, G, B and V optical signals, is presented in Figure 4. The data acquisition was obtained under environment light. On the top the bit sequence used to drive the LEDs is displayed. This sequence allows all the *on/off* sixteen possible combinations of the four input channels ($2^4$).

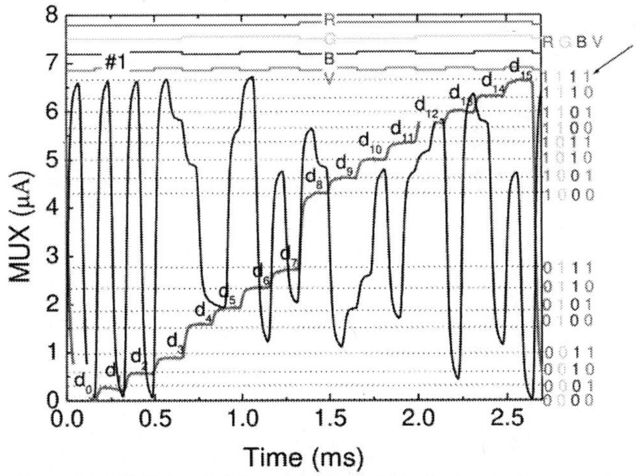


Figure 4. MUX signal of the calibrated cell. On the top the transmitted channels packets [R, G, B, V] are depicted. A received MUX signal is also superimposed to exemplify the decoding process.

Results show that the code signal presents as much separated levels as the *on/off* possible combinations of the input channels, allowing decoding the transmitted information [12]. All the ordered levels ($d_0$-$d_{15}$) are pointed out at the correspondent levels, and are displayed as horizontal dotted lines. In the right hand side the match between MUX levels and the 4 bits binary code assigned to each level is shown. For demonstration of the decoding technique, a signal received, in the same frame of time, when the receiver is in the main the hall (Figure 2a) underneath position #1, is also added. Comparing the calibrated levels ($d_1$-$d_{15}$) with the different assigned 4-digit binary code, the decoding is straightforward.

After decoding each input channel, and taking into account the frame structure (Figure 3), the position of the receiver and its ID in the network is revealed[15] [16]. The footprint position comes directly from the synchronism block, where all the received channels are simultaneously *on* or *off*. For instance, in any footprint #1 the maximum amplitude detected (see arrow) corresponds to the binary word [1111], meaning that the received information comes from the overlap of the four input channels.

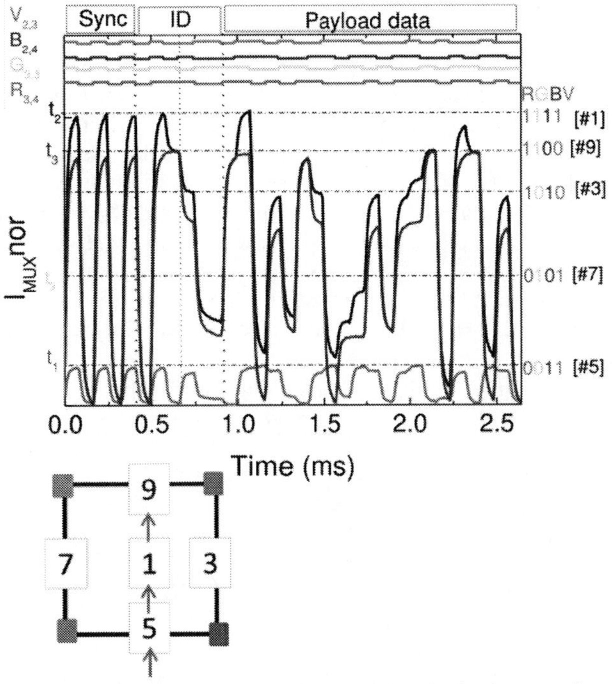


Figure 5. Fine-grained indoor localization and navigation in successive instants (t1, t2 and t3): MUX/DEMUX signals in a point-to-point path across the main hall (#5>#1> #9) at the. On the top the complete transmitted channels packets [R, G, B, V] are decoded.

In Figure 5, for the same frame time and in three successive instants ($t_1$, $t_2$, $t_3$), the received MUX signals, when the receiver is in the main hall and moves from #5 to #9, through #1 (Figure 2a), confirms the decoding process. Decoding, when the four channels overlap (#1), is set on the top of the figure to direct into the packet sent by each node. The footprint position comes directly from the synchronism block. For instance, if the maximum amplitude detected corresponds to the binary word [0011], it means that it has only received the overlap transmission from the blue and the violet channels (footprint #5). In the right side of the figure the levels other levels ascribed to #1, #3, #5 and #9 are point it out.

Each decoded message carries, also, the transmitter's node address. So, the next block of six bits, in the square topology (or eight in the hexagonal one), gives de ID of the received node. In Figure 5, in position #5 the network location of the transmitters are $B_{2,4}$ [010;100] and $V_{2,3}$ [010;011] and while in #1 the assigned transmitters are $R_{3,4}$, $G_{3,3}$, $B_{2,4}$ and $V_{2,3}$. The last block is reserved for the transmission of the advertising (Payload data). The stop bit (0) is used always at the end of each frame.

To compute the point-to-point along a path, we need the data along the path. The input of the aided navigation system is the coded MUX signal, and the output is the system state decoded at each time step ($\Delta t$). As a proof of concept, in the lab, a navigation data bit transition was tested by moving the receiver along known pattern path. In this example (Figure 5) at $t_1$ the user enters the hall by line #5, it goes to position #1 at $t_2$ and it chooses the boarding terminal C (#5) at $t_3$. Results show that, as the receiver moves between generated point regions, the received information pattern changes. Between two consecutive data sets, there is a navigation data bit transition (channel is missing or added). We observe that when the receiver moves from #1 to # 9 (Figure 5) two different ID channels are missing ($B_{2,4}$ and $V_{2,3}$). Here, the 4-bynary bit code has changed from [1111] to [1100].

In Figure 6, a path across the hexagonal topology was also tested. Here, the receiver enters the restaurants area (#4> #5> #3).

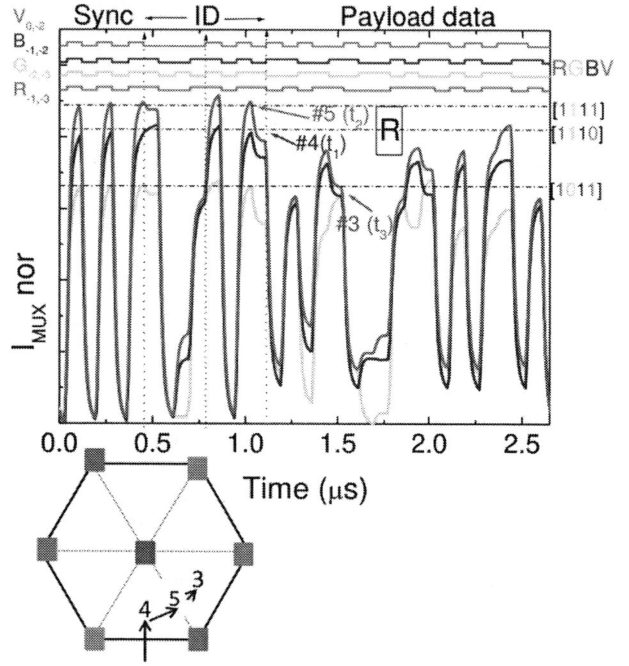


Figure 6 Fine-grained indoor localization and navigation in successive instants instants ($t_1$, $t_2$ and $t_3$). Signal acquisition through the restaurants area (R). On the top the transmitted channels packets are decoded [R, G, B, V].

Main results from both topologies show that fine grained localization is achieved by detecting the wavelengths of the received channels in each region. The location and path of a mobile receiver was obtained based on the LED-based navigation system. In an orthogonal layout (hall), the square topology is the best. It allows crossroads and the client can walk easily in the horizontal, vertical or both directions. In concentric layouts, to fill all the space with hexagon presents advantages (restaurants, and shops areas). Here, the client can move around and walk between the different rings toward the outside region.

## B. *Bidirectional Communication*

The VLC is a wireless broadband technology. It provides multiuser with simultaneous access communication. All the nodes communicate with each other through a centralized controller and the signal is used to establish a point-to-point link between the transmitters and the receiver.

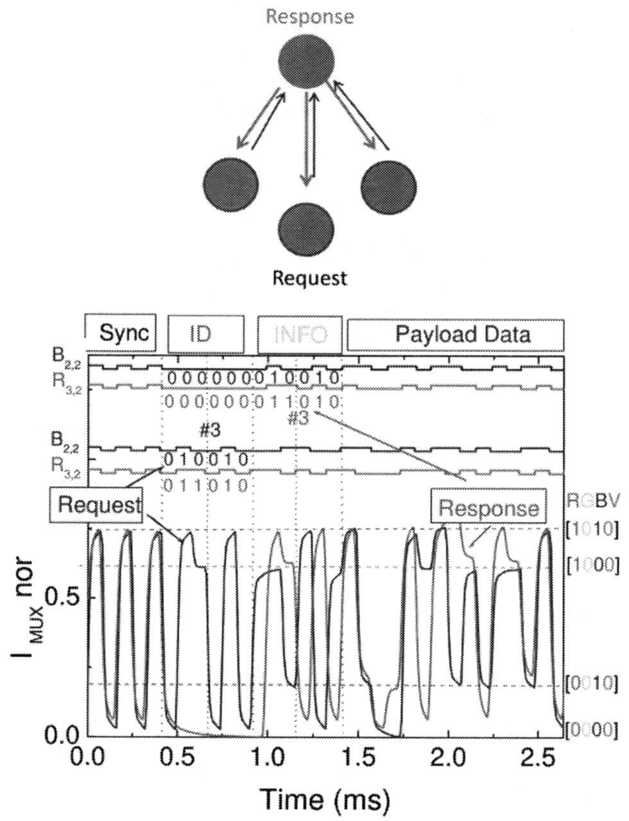


Figure 7. Bidirectional communication: MUX/DEMUX signals assigned to a "request" and a "response" message. On the top the transmitted channels packets [Xi,j] are decoded.

Bidirectional communication between VLC emitters and receivers at a handheld device can be established through a control manager linked to a signboard. Each ceiling lamp broadcasts a message with its ID and useful information which is received and processed by the receiver. Using a white polychromatic LED as optical source for uplink, the receptor sends to the local controller a "request" message with its location (ID) and adds its needs for the available time (Payload data). For route coordination, the local controller emitter sends the downlink "response" message. In Figure 7, the MUX signal assigned to a "request" and a "response" message are displayed. In the top, the decoded information is presented. In the right side, the match between the MUX signal and the 4-binary code is pointed out.

Here, in a time slot, the traveler, in position #3 ($R_{3,2}$ , $B_{2,2}$), sends to the central controller the message "request" in order to add the points of interest (boarding or the right track). After that it is advised, through a "response" message, that the request was received, how to reach its destination in time and how to use location based services. In bidirectional VLC transmission we use different codes in the frame structure for uplink and downlink. Taking into account the frame structure (Figure 3), results show that the codification of both signals is synchronized (Sync). The "request" message includes the complete address of the traveller (Sync+ID) and the help need (Payload Data). In the "response" message the block (ID), in a pattern [000000], means that a response message, from the local manager, is being sent. The next block (6 bits) identifies the address (INFO) for which the message is intended and finally in the last block appears the requested information (Payload Data). Here, the emitter controller [000000] responds to a request of a passenger located in position # 3 ($R_{3,2}$ , $B_{2,2}$) and sends back the requested information.

### C. Multi-person cooperative localization

An unforeseen pandemic is facing the world caused by a corona virus known as SARS-CoV-2. Transmission of the coronavirus is possible indoors, especially when people spend extended periods in crowded and poorly ventilated rooms [ 17 ]. The widely accepted main transmission mechanism is through droplet borne pathways. Person-to-person spread to be the most common form of transmission, occurring mainly among people who are within 2m of each other for a prolonged period of time. This means people should stay the recommended distance apart from others. It also means people should avoid gathering in groups, crowded places and mass gatherings.

Person-to-person spread to be the most common form of transmission of COVID-19, occurring mainly among people who are within 2m of each other for a prolonged period of time. This means people should stay the recommended distance apart from others. It also means people should avoid gathering in groups, crowded places and mass gatherings. So, in crowded building the routes to a specific place should avoid those regions. We consider that the risk of transmission exists if the distance between two users is less than 2 m. The system has to alert the users to stay away from those regions and to plan the better route to the desired wayfinding services

The existence of congested zones can be locally detected by the "mesh / cellular" hybrid controller (Figure 1b), which is also equipped with a modem providing IP base connectivity to the central manager. The hybrid controller integrates the number of requests and individual positions, received during the same time interval. Once the individual positions are known, the relative positions are calculated. If the relative position is less than 2 m, a contamination risk locally exists and an alert message is send for the users and the CM is informed. This alert allows the CM to recalculate, in real time, the best route for the users that request wayfinding services avoiding crowded regions.

## IV. Conclusions

A VLC multi-person cooperative localization dynamic LED-assisted navigation system for large indoor environments was proposed. For lighting, data transmission and positioning, white LEDs were used. A SiC optical MUX/DEMUX mobile receiver decodes the data and based on the synchronism and ID of the joint transmitters infers its location, point-to-point path, timing and user flows.

A VLC scenario was established and the communication protocol presented. Bidirectional communication between the infrastructures and the mobile receivers were analysed. Two cellular networks were tested and compared: square and hexagonal. Main results show that, for both topologies, the location of a mobile receiver, concomitant with data transmission is achieved. The LED-aided VLC navigation system make possible to determine the position of a mobile target inside the network, to infer the travel direction along the time and to interact with received information.

Minding the benefits of VLC, it is expected that this type of communication will have an important role in positioning applications. Moving towards real implementation, the performances of such systems still need to improve. As a future goal, we plan to finalize the embedded application, for experimenting in several network layouts. Effects as synchronization, shadowing and ambient light noise will be minimized by distributing lighting sources (MIMO techniques) to optimize the coverage.

## Acknowledgements

This work was sponsored by FCT – Fundação para a Ciência e a Tecnologia, within the Research Unit CTS – Center of Technology and Systems, reference UIDB/00066/2020. The project IPL/IDI&CA/2020/Geo-Loc/ISEL, is also acknowledge.

## References

[1] C. Yang, and H. R. Shao,, "WiFi-based indoor positioning," IEEE Commun. Mag., vol. 53, no. 3, pp. 150–157, Mar. 2015.

[2] X. Y. Lin, T. W. Ho, C. C. Fang, Z. S. Yen, B.J. Yang, and F. Lai, "A mobile indoor positioning system based on iBeacon technology," in Proc. Int. Conf. IEEE Eng. Med. Biol. Soc., pp. 4970–4973, 2015.

[3] C. H. Huang, L. H. Lee, C. C. Ho, L. L. Wu, and Z. H. Lai, "Real-time rfid indoor positioning system based on kalman filter drift removal and heron-bilateration location estimation," IEEE Trans. Instrum. Meas., vol. 64, no. 3, pp. 728–739, Mar. 2015.

[4] N. U. Hassan, A. Naeem, M. A. Pasha, T. Jadoon, and C. Yuen, "Indoor positioning using visible led lights: A survey,"ACM Comput. Surv., vol. 48, pp. 1–32 , 2015.

[5] E. Ozgur E. Dinc, O. B. Akan, "Communicate to illuminate: State-of-the-art and research challenges for visible light communications," Physical Communication 17 pp. 72–85, 2015.

[6] D. Tsonev, H. Chun, S. Rajbhandari, J. McKendry, S. Videv, E. Gu, M. Haji, S. Watson, A. Kelly, G. Faulkner, M., Dawson, H. Haas, and D. O'Brien, "A 3-Gb/s single-LED OFDM-based wireless VLC link using a Gallium Nitride µLED," IEEE Photon. Technol. Lett. 26 (7), pp.637–640, 2014.

[7] D. O'Brien, H. L. Minh, L. Zeng, G. Faulkner, K. Lee, D. Jung, Y. Oh, and E. T. Won, "Indoor visible light communications: challenges and prospects," Proc. SPIE 7091, 709106, 2008.

[8] M. Vieira, P. Louro, M. Fernandes, M. A. Vieira, A. Fantoni and J. Costa, "Three Transducers Embedded into One Single SiC Photodetector: LSP Direct Image Sensor, Optical Amplifier and Demux Device," Advances in Photodiodes InTech, Chap.19, pp.403-425, 2011.

[9] M. A. Vieira, P. Louro, M. Vieira, A. Fantoni, and A. Steiger-Garção, "Light-activated amplification in Si-C tandem devices: A capacitive active filter model," IEEE sensor journal, 12, NO. 6, pp. 1755-1762, 2012.

[10] A. Jovicic, J. Li, and T. Richardson, "Visible light communication: opportunities, challenges and the path to market," Communications Magazine, IEEE, vol. 51, no. 12, pp. 26–32, 2013.

[11] S. B. Park, D. K.Jung, H. S. Shing, D. J. Shing, Y. J. Hyun, K. Li, and Y. J. Oh, "Information broadcasting system based on visible light signboard," presented at Wireless and Optical Communication 2007, Montreal, Canada, 2007.

[12] A. Yousefpour C. Fung T. Nguyen, K. Kadiyala, F. Jalali, A. Niakanlahiji, J. Kong J. P. Jue, "All one needs to know about fog computing and related edge computing paradigms: A complete survey", Journal of Systems Architecture,Volume 98, pp. 289-330, 2019.

[13] M. Vieira, M. A. Vieira., P. Louro., P. Vieira, A. Fantoni, "Fine-grained indoor localization: optical sensing and detection," Proc. SPIE 10680, Optical Sensing and Detection V, 106800H (9 May 2018).

[14] M. Vieira, M. A. Vieira., P. Louro., P. Vieira, A. Fantoni,., "Light-emitting diodes aided indoor localization using visible light communication technology," Opt. Eng. 57(8), 087105 (2018).

[15] M. A. Vieira, M. Vieira, P. Louro,V. Silva, and P. Vieira, , "Optical signal processing for indoor positioning using a-SiCH technology," Opt. Eng. 55 (10), 107105, 2016.

[16] M. Vieira, M: A. Vieira, P. Louro, and Vieira, "Positioning and advertising in large indoor environments using visible light communication," Opt. Eng. 58(6), 066102, 2019.

[17] C. Iddon, A. Hathaway and S. Fitzgerald S., "CIBSE COVID-19 Ventilation Guidance", CIBSE, 2020.

# Visible Light Communication in a Traffic Controlled Split Intersection

Manuel Augusto Vieira, Manuela Vieira, Paula Louro
ADETC/ISEL/IPL,
R. Conselheiro Emídio Navarro, 1959-007
Lisboa, Portugal
CTS-UNINOVA
Quinta da Torre, Monte da Caparica, 2829-516,
Caparica, Portugal

e-mail: mv@isel.pt, mv@ipl.isel.pt, plouro@deetc.isel.pt,
afantoni@deetc.isel.ipl.pt

Pedro Vieira
ADETC/ISEL/IPL,
R. Conselheiro Emídio Navarro, 1959-007
Lisboa, Portugal
Instituto das Telecomunicações
Instituto Superior Técnico, 1049-001,
Lisboa, Portugal
e-mail: pvieira@isel.pt

***Abstract*— In order to serve the changing needs of road traffic control, the road space and road structure surrounding an intersection have evolved into complex forms. The redesign or split of the trajectories though complex, can be accomplished by the application of methods for navigation, guidance and combination of expert knowledge of road traffic control of vehicles. A proposed innovative treatment for congested urban is the split intersection. It facilitates a smoother flow with less driver delay by reducing the number of vehicle signal phases. The success of converting to the split intersection is analyzed by using microsimulation. A phasing traffic flow is developed as a proof of concept. A Vehicle-to-Everything (V2X) traffic scenario is stablished and the experimental results confirm the cooperative Visible Light Communication (VLC) architecture showing that communication between connected bicycles and motor vehicles is optimized using a request/response concept. In this work, the communication between the infrastructures and the bicycles and motor vehicles, between vehicles and from the bicycles and motor vehicles to the infrastructures is performed through Visible Light Communication (VLC) using the street lamps and the traffic signaling to broadcast the information. Data is encoded, modulated and converted into light signals emitted by the transmitters. Tetra-chromatic white sources are used providing a different data channel for each chip. As receivers and decoders, SiC Wavelength Division Multiplexer (WDM) optical sensor, with light filtering properties, are used. The primary objective is to control the arrival of vehicles to an intersection and to schedule them to cross it at times that minimizes delays. A Vehicle-to-Everything (V2X) traffic scenario is stablished and bidirectional communication between the infrastructure and the vehicles is tested, using the VLC request/response concept.**

***Keywords- Vehicular Communication; Light Fidelity; Visible Light Communication; white LEDs; SiC photodetectors; OOK modulation scheme;Traffic control.***

## I. INTRODUCTION

The Visible Light Communication (VLC) holds special importance when compared to existing forms of wireless communications [1] [2]. VLC seems to be appropriate for providing wireless data exchange for automotive applications. Visible light represents a new communication opportunity for vehicular networking applications. The communication is performed through VLC using the street lamps and the traffic signaling to broadcast the information.

An Intersection Manager (IM) can increase the throughput of the intersection by exchanging information with and directing incoming Connected Autonomous Vehicles [3][4][ 5]

Our goal is to increase the safety and throughput of traffic intersections using VLC connected cooperative driving [6][7]. Vehicular Communication Systems are a type of network in which vehicles and roadside units are the communicating nodes, providing each other with information, such as safety warnings and traffic information [8]. Communication between fixed locations and vehicles (Infrastructure-to-Vehicle, I2V) between vehicles (Vehicle-to-Vehicle, V2V), and between vehicles and fixed locations (Vehicle-to-Infrastructure, V2I) is essential to transfer information in real time. The I2V applications focus on utilizing the traffic related infrastructure, such as traffic light or streetlight to communicate useful information.

The proposed system is composed of several transmitters, i.e., the street lights and the traffic signals, which transmit map information and traffic messages required to the moving vehicles. Data is encoded, modulated and converted into light signals emitted by the transmitters. Then, this information is transferred to receivers installed in the vehicles. Every street light has their differentiable Identifications (IDs) for the generation of the visible light signal that transmits the map information through a Visible Light Transmitter module. Tetra-chromatic white sources are used providing a different data channel for each chip. Every vehicle is equipped with a receiver module for receiving the mapped information generated from the street. The receiver modules include a photodetector based on a tandem a-SiC:H/a-Si:H pin/pin light controlled filter [9][10][11] that multiplex the different optical channels, perform different filtering processes (amplification, switching, and wavelength conversion) and decode the encoded signals, recovering the transmitted information.

This paper is organized as follows: After a short introduction, in Section II, a two-way communication between vehicles and the traffic lights is implemented. The redesign of the trajectory is presented. Here, street lamps and traffic lights broadcast the information. The On-vehicle VLC receivers decode the messages and perform V2V distance measurements. In Section III, a V2X traffic scenario is proposed and characterized. A phasing traffic flow is developed as a Proof-of-Concept (PoC). The simulated results confirm that the redesign of the intersection and its management through the cooperative request/response VLC architecture allows to increase the safety and to decrease the trip delay. Finally in Section IV, the main conclusions are presented.

## II. VEHICULAR COMMUNICATION USING VLC

In this section the vehicular communication is analyzed.

### A. *Redesign Concepts*

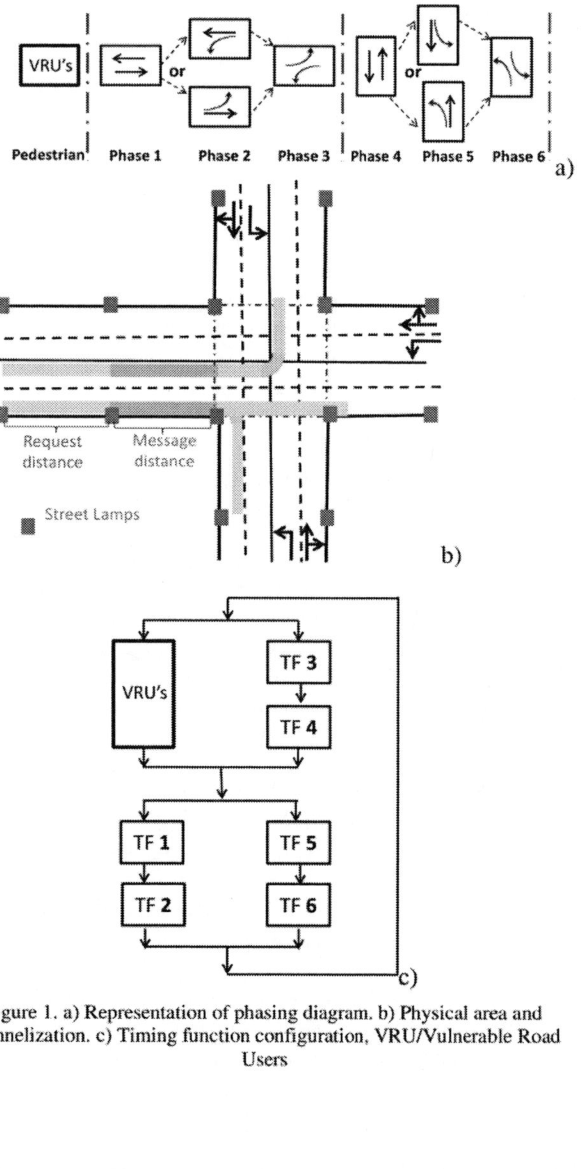


Figure 1. a) Representation of phasing diagram. b) Physical area and channelization. c) Timing function configuration, VRU/Vulnerable Road Users

The redesign of the traffic-actuated controller uses vehicle request/respond message information to generate phase durations appropriate to accommodate the demand on each cycle. Examples of the representation of a redesigned phasing diagram, a functional area with two-way-two-way intersection and a timing function configuration are presented in Figure 1. In Figure 1a, a phasing diagram is displayed. Each Timing Function (TF) controls only one movement represented by an arrow. Since two movements can proceed simultaneously without conflict as shown in Figure 1b, hence two of the timing functions will always have simultaneous control, as exemplified in Figure 1c. The problem that the traffic-actuated intersection manager has to solve is to allocate the reservations among a set of drivers in a way that a specific objective is maximized. Signal timing involves the determination of the appropriate cycle length and apportionment of time among competing movements and phases. The timing apportionment is constrained by minimum "green" times that must be imposed to provide pedestrians to cross and to ensure that motorist expectancy is not violated.

The use of both navigation and lane control signs to communicate lane restrictions is demanding. Downstream from that location (request distance in Figure 1b), lane restrictions should be obeyed. Vehicles may receive their requirements (*e.g.*, whether they will turn left or continue straight and turn right) or the need to interact with a trafic controler at a nearby crossroad (message distance in Figure 1b). In the sequence, a traffic message coming from a transmitter nearby the crossroad will inform the drivers of the location of their destination (*i.e.*, the intended intersection exit leg).

### B. *V2X communication scenario .*

A V2X (I2V2V2I2V) communication link, in a light traffic controlled crossroad, was simulated. The crossroad link is displayed in Figure 2. In the PoC, was assumed that the crossroad in an orthogonal configuration is located in the interception of line 2 with column 3, and the emitters at the nodes along the roadside.

To build the I2V it is proposed a simplified cluster of unit square cells in an orthogonal topology that fills all the service area [13]. To realize both the communication and the street illumination, white light tetra-chromatic sources are used providing a different data channel for each chip. At each node, only one chip of the LED is modulated for data transmission, the Red (R: 626 nm), the Green (G: 530 nm), the Blue (B: 470 nm) or the Violet (V) while the others provide constant current for white perception. Thus, each transmitter, $X_{i,j}$, carries its own color, X, (RGBV) as well as its horizontal and vertical ID position in the surrounding network (*i,j*).

The VLC photosensitive receiver is a double pin/pin photodetector based on a tandem heterostructure, p-i'(a -SiC:H)-n/p-i(a-Si:H)-n. [ 12 ][ 13 ]). To receive the I2V information from several transmitters, the receiver must be located at the overlap of the circles that set the transmission range of each transmitter.

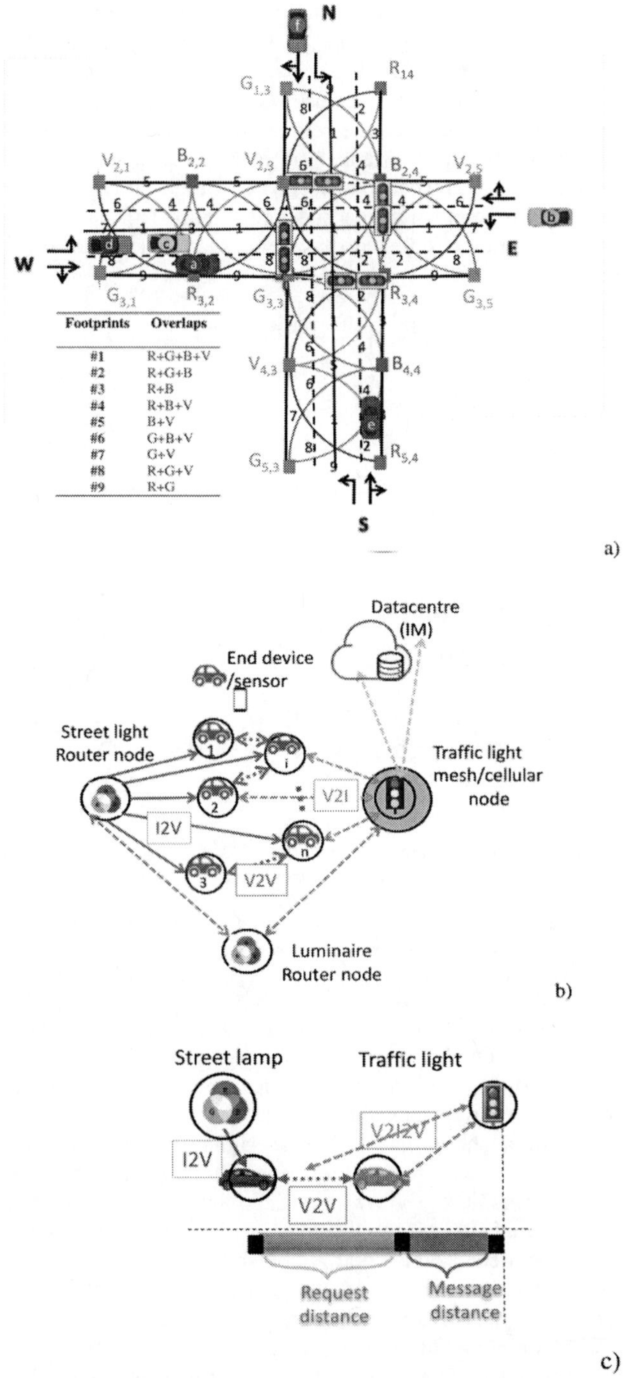


Figure.2.a) V2X lighting plan model and generated joint footprints in a crossroad (LED array=RGBV color spots). b) Proposed mesh and cellular hybrid architecture.

The nine possible overlaps are displayed in Figure 2a for each unit square cell. When a probe vehicle enters the streetlight´s capture range, the receiver replies to the light signal, and assigns an unique ID and the traffic message [14].In Figure 2b, we propose a draft of a mesh cellular hybrid structure to create a gateway-less system without any external gateways needed. We propose this network configuration since it is wireless and ad-hoc. It spans all devices, is wire free, demonstrates resiliency to physical obstructions and adapts to changes in the transmission medium. Therefore, a mesh network is a good fit because it dynamically reconfigures itself and grows to the size of any installation. Is also a secure and trustworthy network [15]. As illustrated in Figure 2b, the street lights, in this architecture, are equipped with one of two types of nodes: A "mesh" controller that connects with other nodes in its vicinity (solid arrows). These controllers can forward messages to the vehicles (I2V) in the mesh, effectively acting like routers nodes in the network. The "mesh/cellular" hybrid controller (dash arrows), is also equipped with a modem providing IP base connectivity to the Intersection Manager services (IM). These nodes acts as border-router and can be used for edge computing. Under this architecture, the short-range mesh network purpose is twofold: enable edge computing and device-to-cloud communication, by ensuring a secure communication from a street light controller to the edge computer or datacenter, through a neighbor traffic light controller with an active cellular connection; and enable peer-to-peer communication, to exchange information between V-VLC ready connected cars.

Four traffic flows were considered: One from West (W) with three vehicles ("a", "c", "d") approaching the crossroad, Vehicle *a* with straight movement and Vehicle *c* and Vehicle *d* with left turn only. In the second flow, Vehicle *b* from East (E), approaches the interception with left turn only. In the third flow, Vehicle *e*, oncoming from South (S), has e right-turn approach. Finally, in the fourth flow, Vehicle *f*, coming from North, goes straight. Using the I2V communication, each street lamp (transmitter) sends a message, which is received and processed by a SiC receiver, located at the vehicle's rooftop. Using the headlights as transmitters, the information is resent to a leader vehicle (V2V) or, depending on the predefined occupied lane, a "request" message to go forward or turn right (right lane) or to turn left (left lane) is sent directly to a crossroad receiver (V2I), at the traffic light, interconnected to a local manager that feeds one or more signal heads. For crossroad coordination, a emitting local controller located at the light signal, sends a "response" message to the intersection approaching vehicles. In the following, bidirectional communication is stablished (V2I2V).

To build the V2V system, the follower sends the message that is received by the leader and can be retransmitted to the next car [16][17] or to the infrastructure. The leader vehicle receives infers the drive distance and the relative speed between them [18]. This information can be directed to the next car (V2V) or to an infrastructure (V2I).

For the intersection manager crossing coordination, the vehicle and the intersection manager exchange information through two specific types of messages, "request" (V2I) and "response" (I2V). Inside the request distance, an approach "request" is sent, using as emitter the headlights. To receive the "requests", two different receivers are located at the same traffic light, facing the cross roads (local controller of the traffic light). The "request" contains all the information that is necessary for a vehicle's space-time reservation for its intersection crossing. Intersection manager uses this information to convert it in a sequence of timed rectangular spaces that each assigned vehicle needs to occupy the intersection. An intersection manager's acknowledgement is sent from the traffic signal over the facing receiver to the in car application of the head vehicle. The response includes both the infrastructure and the vehicle identifications and the "confirmed vehicle" message. Once the response is received (message distance in Figure 1b), the vehicle is required to follow the occupancy trajectories (footprint regions, Figure 2) provided by the intersection manager. If a request has any potential risk of collision with all other vehicles that have already been approved to cross the intersection, the control manager only sends back to the vehicle (V2I) the "response" after the risk of conflict is exceeded.

The graphical representation of the simultaneous localization and mapping problem, for the V2X communication link, is displayed in Figure 2c. Here, using the I2V communication, each street lamp (transmitter) sends a message, which is received and processed by a SiC receiver, located at the vehicle's rooftop. Using the headlights as transmitters, the information is resent to a leader vehicle (V2V) [ 19 ][ 20 ] or, depending on the predefined occupied lane, a "request" message to go forward or turn right (right lane) or to turn left (left lane) is sent directly to a crossroad receiver (V2I), at the traffic light, interconnected to a local manager that feeds one or more signal heads. This information can be directed to the next car (V2V) or to an infrastructure (V2I). For crossroad coordination, an emitting local controller located at the light signal, send a "response" message to the intersection approaching vehicles. In the following, bidirectional communication is stablished (V2I2V).

### C. *Coding/decoding Techniques*

To encode the messages an on-off keying (OOK) modulation scheme was used. The codification of the optical signals is synchronized and includes the information related to the ID position of the transmitters and the message to broadcast. We have considered a 32 bits codification as described in Figure 3.

Each frame is divided into three or four blocks depending on the kind of transmitter: street lamps, headlamps (Figure 3a) or traffic light (Figure 3b). We assigned the first block to the synchronization (SYNC) in a [10101] pattern and the last one to the message to transmit (Payload Data). A stop bit is used at the end of each frame. Thus, $R_{3,2}$, $G_{3,1}$, and $V_{21}$ are the transmitted node packets, in a time slot by the headlamps. In Figure 3b, the second block (INFO) in a pattern [000000] means that a response message is being sent by the controller manager. Here, the signal controller responds to the request of the vehicle located in position # 8 ($R_{3,2}$, $G_{3,3}$, and $V_{23}$) at the request time (request distance). This response is received in the unit cell adjacent to the crossroad (message distance, Figure 1b) that shares a common node ($R_{3,2}$) with the request distance (see Figure 3).

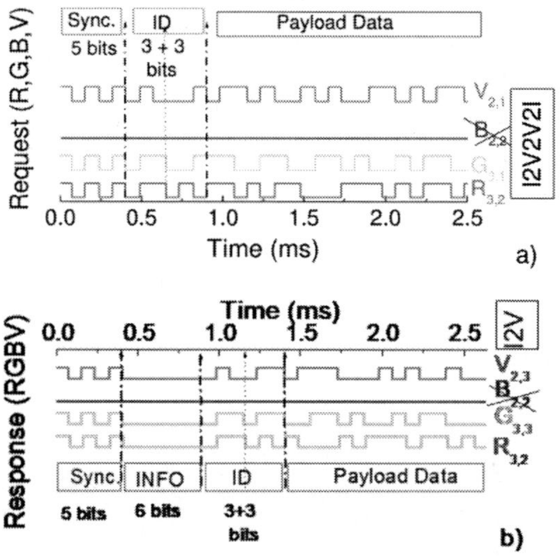


Figure 3. Frame structure representations. a) Codification used to drive the headlights of a vehicle in a request message from footprint #8. $R_{3,2}$, $G_{3,1}$, and $V_{2,1}$ are the transmitted node packet, in a time slot .b) Encoded message response of the controller to the request message of the vehicle in position #8 ($R_{3,2}$, $G_{3,1}$, and $V_{2,1}$).

In Figure 4, a MUX signal due to the joint transmission of four R, G, B and V optical signals, in a data frame, is displayed. The bit sequence (on the top of the figure) was chosen to allow all the *on/off* sixteen possible combinations of the four input channels ($2^4$).

Results show that the code signal presents as much separated levels as the *on/off* possible combinations of the input channels, allowing decoding the transmitted information [9]. All the levels ($d_0$-$d_{15}$) are pointed out at the correspondent levels, and displayed as horizontal dotted lines. In the right hand side, the match between MUX levels and the 4 bits binary code assigned to each level is shown. To exemplify of the decoding technique, the signal transmitted in Figure 3a in the same frame of time, is also added (dotted curve).

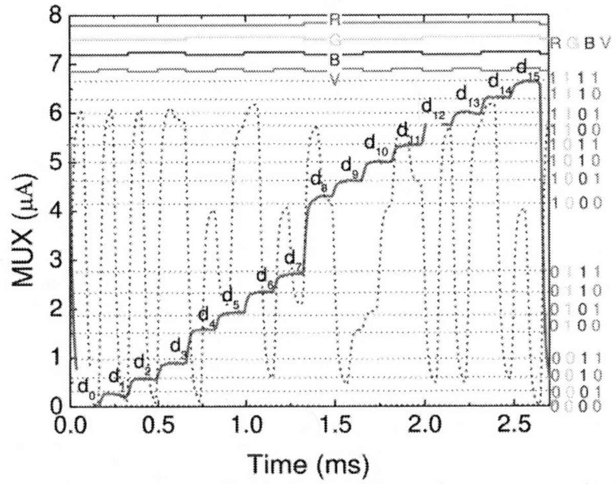


Figure 4. MUX signal of the calibrated cell. On the top the transmitted channels packets [R, G, B, V] are depicted. A received MUX signal is also superimposed to exemplify the decoding algorithm.

Hence, the signal can be decoded by assigning each output level ($d_0$-$d_{15}$) to a 4- digit binary code [$X_R$, $X_G$, $X_B$, $X_V$], with X=1 if the channel is *on* and X=0 if it is *off*.

## III. RESULTS

Main results are presented and discussed.

### A. Led assisted navigation

As a PoC, performed in the lab, a navigation data bit transition was tested by moving the receiver along known pattern path as shown in Figure 5.

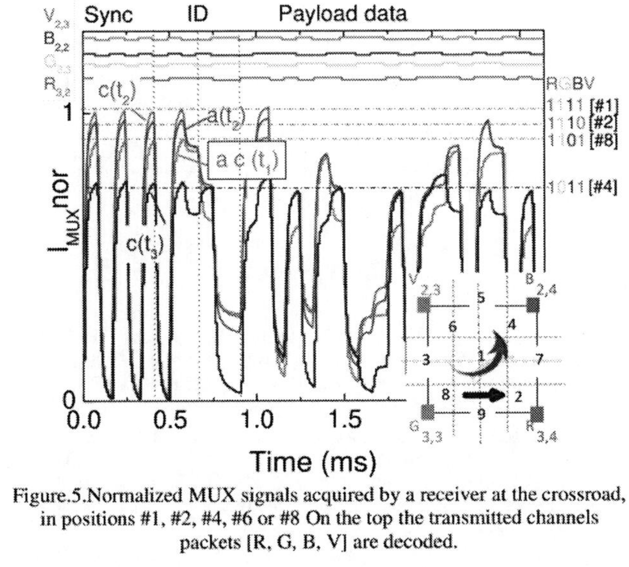


Figure.5.Normalized MUX signals acquired by a receiver at the crossroad, in positions #1, #2, #4, #6 or #8 On the top the transmitted channels packets [R, G, B, V] are decoded.

Figure 5, displays the MUX signals received when Vehicle *a* enters the crossroad in position #8 ($t_1$) and it goes straight to position #2 ($t_2$) (Phase1, TF1) , while vehicle *c* turn left, moving across position #1 (Phase2, TF2). Results show that, as the receiver moves between generated point regions, the received information pattern changes. The vehicle speed can be calculated by measuring the actual travelled distance overtime, using the ID´s transmitters tracking. Between two consecutive data sets, there is a navigation data bit transition (channel is missing or added). It was observed that when the receiver moves from #8 to # 2 one ID channels was lost ($B_{2,4}$) and one are added ($V_{2,3}$). Here, the 4-bynary bit code has changed from [1101] to [1110] while Vehicle *c* and *d* change theirs from [1111] to [0011] and Vehicle *b* to [1100]. The receivers compute the geographical position in the successive instants (path) and infer the vehicle's speed. In the following, this data will be transmitted to another leader vehicle through the V2V communication or to control manager at the traffic light through V2I.

### B. Cooperative system

To model the worst-case scenario, vehicles approaching the intersection from different flows are assumed to have a conflicting trajectory (Figure 2). Two instants are considered for each vehicle, the request time (t) and the response time (t'). All the requests contain vehicle positions and approach speeds. If a follower exists (Vehicle *d*), the request message from its leader includes the position and speed previously received by V2V. This information alerts the controller to a later request message (V2I), confirmed by the follow vehicle. In the PoC we have assumed that $t_a < t_c < t_d$, and $t_a < t_b < t_c$.

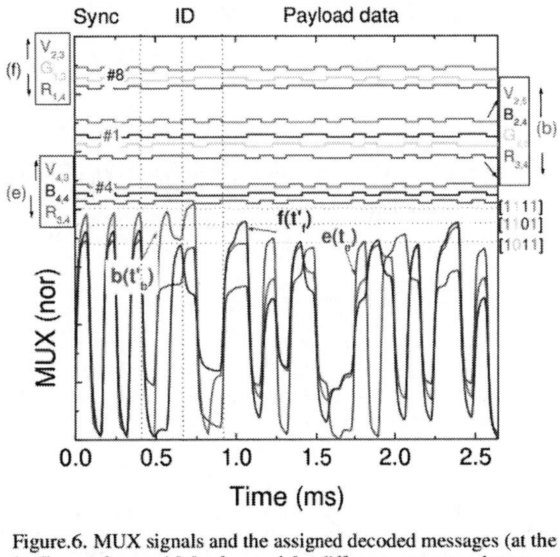


Figure.6. MUX signals and the assigned decoded messages (at the top of the figure) from vehicles *b*, *e* and *f* at different request and response times (I2V).

As an example, in Figure 6, the I2V MUX signals received and decode (on the top of the figure) by the receivers of the vehicles *b*, *e* and *f* are also displayed at request ($t_e$) and ($t'_b$ and $t'_f$) response times. In the right side, the received channels for each vehicle are identified by its 4-digit binary codes and associated positions in the unit cel

After decoding we have assigned position #4 ($R_{3,4}$ $G_{4,4}$ $V_{4,3}$) for Vehicle *e*, position #1 ($R_{3,4}$ $G_{3,5}$ $B_{2,4}$ $V_{2,5}$) for Vehicle *b* and position #8 ($R_{1,4}$ $G_{1,3}$ $V_{2,3}$) to Vehicle *f* , respectively at theirs request and response times $t_e$ , $t'_b$ and $t'_f$ . Here, $t'_e<t'_f$.

### C. *Traffic Signal Phasing in a V2X Communication*

A phasing diagram and a timing function configuration were presented in Figure 1, for functional areas with two-way-two-way intersection. A traffic scenario was simulated (Figure 2) using the new concept of VLC request/response messages. A brief look into the process of timing traffic signals is given in Figure 7.

Redesign traffic-actuated controller uses *a, b, c, d, e* and *f* vehicles requesting and responding message information to generate phase durations appropriate to accommodate the demand on each cycle. Each driving vehicle is assigned an individualised time to request (*t*) and access (*t'*) the intersection. The exclusive pedestrian stage, "Walk" interval begins at the end of Phase 5. (Figure 1).

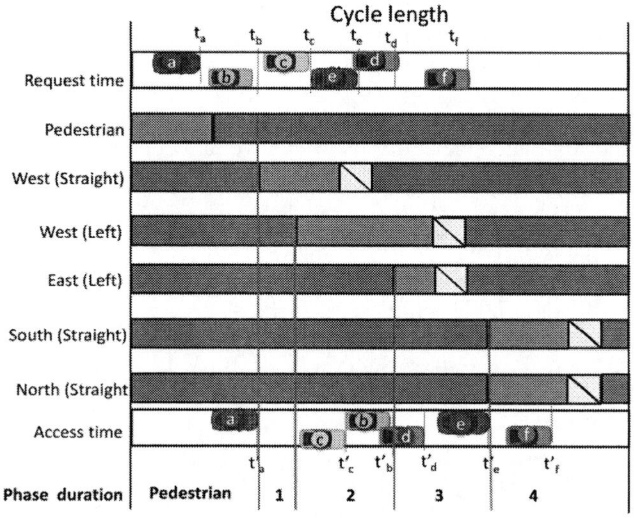


Figure. 7 Requested phasing of traffic flows: pedestrian phase, Phase 1 (W straight flow), Phase 2 (W straight and left flows), Phase 3(W and E left flows), Phase 4 (N and S straight flows). $t_{[x]}$ is the request time from the Vehicle *x* and $t'_{[X]}$ the correspondent response time from the manage controller.

A first-come-first-serve approach could be realized by accelerating or decelerating the vehicles such that they arrive at the intersection when gaps in the conflicting traffic flows and pedestrians have been created. However, a one-by-one service policy at high vehicle arrival rates is not efficient. From the capacity point of view, it is more efficient, if Vehicle *c* is given access at $t'_c$ before Vehicle *b*, at $t'_b$ to the intersection and Vehicle *d* is given access at $t'_d$ before Vehicle *e*, at $t'_e$ then, forming a west left turn of set of vehicles (platoon) before giving way to the fourth phase (north and south conflicting flows), as stated in Figure 7The speed of Vehicle *e* was reduced, keeping a safe distance between Vehicle *e* and Vehicle *d*.

## IV. CONCLUSIONS

This paper presents a new concept of request/response for the redesign and management of a trajectory in a two-way-two-way traffic lights controlled crossroad, using VLC between connected cars. The connected vehicles receive information from the network (I2V), interact with each other (V2V) and also with the infrastructure (V2I), using the request redesign distance concept. In parallel, a control manager coordinates the crossroad and interacts with the vehicles (I2V) using the response redesign distance concept. A simulated traffic scenario was presented and a generic model of cooperative transmission for vehicular communication services was established. As a PoC, a phasing of traffic flows is suggested. The simulated/experimental results confirmed that the proposed cooperative VLC architecture is suitable for the intended applications. The introduction of VLC between connected vehicles and the surrounding infrastructure allows the direct monitoring of relative speed thresholds and inter-vehicle spacing.

In order to evolve towards real implementation, the performance of such systems still needs improvement, namely the distance between conflicting vehicles along with the trajectories of other opposing vehicles should also be monitored and optimized. As further work, the research team plans to finalize the embedded application, for experimenting in several road configurations with either static or moving vehicles.

## ACKNOWLEDGEMENTS

This work was sponsored by FCT – Fundação para a Ciência e a Tecnologia, within the Research Unit CTS – Center of Technology and systems, reference UIDB/00066/2020. The project IPL/IDI&CA/2020/Geo-Loc/ISEL, are also acknowledge.

## REFERENCES

[1] D. O'Brien, H. L Minh, L. Zeng, G. Faulkner, K Lee, D. Jung, Y. Oh, and E. T. Won, "Indoor Visible Light Communications: challenges and prospects," Proc. SPIE 7091, 709106 (2008).

[2] H. Pathak, F. Xiaotao, H. Pengfei, and M. Prasant, "Visible Light Communication, Networking and Sensing: Potential and Challenges," September 2015, IEEE Communications Surveys & Tutorials 17(4): Fourthquarter 2015, pp. 2047 – 2077 (2015).

[3] D. Elliott,W. Keen, and L. Miao, "Recent advances in connected and automated vehicles" Journal of Traffic and Transportation Engineering, Vol. 6, Issue 2, pp.109-131(April 2019).

[4] N. Jitendra, Bajpai, "Emerging vehicle technologies & the search for urban mobility solutions,Urban, Planning and TransportResearch, 4:1, pp.83-100, DOI: 10.1080/21650020.2016.1185964(2016).

[5] N. Wang, Y. Qiao, W. Wang, S. Tang, and J. Shen, "Visible Light Communication based Intelligent Traffic Light System: Designing and Implementation,"2018 Asia Communications and Photonics Conference (ACP) DOI: 10.1109/ACP.2018.8595791(2018).

[6] N. Cheng, F. Lyu, J. Chen, W. Xu, H. Zhou, S. Zhang, and X. S. Shen, "Big data driven vehicular networks," IEEE Network, vol. 32, no. 6, pp.160–167, (Nov. 2018).

[7] P. Singh, G. Singh, and A. Singh, "Implementing Visible Light Communication in intelligent traffic management to resolve traffic logjams,"-Int. J. Comput. Eng. Res., 2015 - academia.edu (2015).

[8] S. Yousefi, E. Altman, R. El-Azouzi, and M. Fathy, "Analytical Model for Connectivity in Vehicular Ad Hoc Networks," IEEE Transactions on Vehicular Technology, 57, pp.3341-3356 (2008).

[9] M. Vieira, P. Louro, M. Fernandes, M. A. Vieira, A. Fantoni and J. Costa, "Three Transducers Embedded into One Single SiC Photodetector: LSP Direct Image Sensor, Optical Amplifier and Demux Device," Advances in Photodiodes InTech, Chap.19, pp.403-425 (2011).

[10] M. A. Vieira, P. Louro, M. Vieira, A. Fantoni, and A. Steiger-Garção, "Light-activated amplification in Si-C tandem devices: A capacitive active filter model," IEEE sensor journal, 12( 6), 1755-1762 (2012).

[11] M. A. Vieira, M. Vieira, P., Vieira, and P. Louro, "Optical signal processing for a smart vehicle lighting system using a-SiCH technology," Proc. SPIE 10231, Optical Sensors 2017, 102311L (2017);

[12] M. A. Vieira, M. Vieira, V. Silva, P. Louro, and J Costa, "Optical signal processing for data error detection and correction using a-SiCH technology," Phys. Status Solidi C 12 ( 12), pp.1393–1400 (2015).

[13] M. A. Vieira, M. Vieira, P. Louro, and P. Vieira, "Bi-directional communication between infrastructures and vehicles through visible light," Proc. SPIE 11207, Fourth International Conference on Applications of Optics and Photonics, 112070C (3 October 2019); doi: 10.1117/12.2526500 (2019).

[14] M. A. Vieira, M. Vieira, P. Vieira, and P. Louro, "Vehicle-to-Vehicle and Infrastructure-to-Vehicle Communication in the Visible Range," Sensors & Transducers, 218 (12), pp.40-48 (2017)

[15] A. Yousefpour, C. Fung, T. Nguyen, K. Kadiyala, F. Jalali, A. Niakanlahiji, J. Kong, and J. P. Jue.,"All one needs to know about fog computing and related edge computing paradigms: A complete survey", Journal of Systems Architecture,Volume 98, pp. 289-330 (2019).

[16] M. A. Vieira, M. Vieira, P. Louro, and P. Vieira, "Smart Vehicle Lighting System in the Visible Range: Vehicle-to-Vehicle Communication," The Eighth International Conference on Sensor Device Technologies and Applications. SENSORDEVICES 2017. - Rome, Italy. Copyright (c) IARIA ISBN: 978-1-61208-581-4, pp.57-62 (2017).

[17] .M. A.Vieira; M. Vieira; P. Vieira; and P. Louro, "Optical signal processing for a smart vehicle lighting system using a-SiCH technology," Proc. SPIE. 10231 Optical Sensors 2017, 102311L. (2017).

[18] M. A. Vieira; M. Vieira; P. Vieira; and P. Louro,. "Cooperative vehicular communication systems based on visible light communication," Opt. Eng. 57(7), 076101 (2018).

[19] M. A.Vieira; M. Vieira; P. Vieira; and P. Louro, "Optical signal processing for a smart vehicle lighting system using a-SiCH technology," Proc. SPIE. 10231 Optical Sensors 2017, 102311L. (2017).

[20] M. A. Vieira; M. Vieira; P. Vieira; and P.Louro, "Cooperative vehicular communication systems based on visible light communication," Opt. Eng. 57(7), 076101 (2018).

# Propagation Model Using White LEDs in a Visible Light Communication Link

Paula Louro, Manuela Vieira, Manuel A. Vieira,
ADEETC/ISEL/IPL
R. Conselheiro Emídio Navarro, 1
1959-007 Lisboa, Portugal
CTS-UNINOVA
Quinta da Torre, Monte da Caparica, 2829-516, Caparica, Portugal
e-mail: plouro@deetc.isel.pt, mv@isel.ipl.pt, mvieira@deetc.isel.ipl.pt

Pedro Vieira
ADEETC/ISEL/IPL
R. Conselheiro Emídio Navarro, 1
1959-007 Lisboa, Portugal
Instituto das Telecomunicações
IST, Av. Rovisco Pais,
1049-001 Lisboa, Portugal
e-mail: pedro.vieira@isel.pt

***Abstract*—Nowadays, Global Positioning Systems (GPS) are used everywhere for positioning and navigation. However, its use is not suitable in indoor environment, due to the strong attenuation inside buildings. Therefore, indoors navigation takes advantage of other technologies to infer position. Recently, several Visible Light Positioning (VLP) systems have been reported. Among these technologies, Visible Light Communication (VLC) is one of the most promising, as its operation is based on the use of Light Emitting Diode (LED) light, currently widely used in the illumination solutions of most buildings. In this paper, we propose an indoor navigation system based on VLC in an industrial application for automated warehouses, where the navigation of Autonomous Guided Vehicles (AGV) is supported by VLC. The proposed VLC system establishes bi-directional communication between the infrastructure and the guided vehicles. LED transmitters at the warehouse ceiling support downlink data transmission from the Infrastructure to Vehicle (I2V). This channel provides positioning and navigation of the vehicles, as well as transmission of dedicated messages related to the requested tasks of the management warehouse system to the AVGs. The uplink channel from the Vehicle to the Infrastructure (V2I) is used to acknowledge the requested tasks and transmit updates on the concluded tasks. Optical transmitters are tri-chromatic white LEDs with a wide angle beam. The characterization of the optical transmitter system is done through MatLab simulations for path loss and VLC channel gain prediction using the Lambertian model for the LED light distribution. Dedicated receivers based on a-SiC:H/a-Si:H photodiodes with selective spectral sensitivity are used to record the transmitted signal. The decoding strategy is based on accurate calibration of the output signal.**

***Keywords - visible light communication; RGB LED; photodiode; indoor navigation; optical sensor.***

## I. INTRODUCTION

Visible Light Communication (VLC) technology makes use of the visible part of the light spectrum to modulate specific wavelengths and encode and transmit information [1]. White LED lamps are the most adequate transmitters in this technology, as white LEDs are currently the most efficient lighting solution and can also be easily modulated, fulfilling the VLC requirements for signal transmission [2][3]. An attractive application of VLC technology is for indoor positioning and navigation services [4]. Its use can be extended from in-house navigation to guide users inside large buildings or underground spaces to the navigation of AVGs, safe communication at RF hazardous places (petrochemical industries, mining) [5] or RF undesirable locations (hospitals, aircrafts) [6][7].

Nowadays, retail market has several online and offline channels of sales and services like same day delivery or store pickups [8]. Thus, the trend for the conception of modern warehousing has provide efficiency in the delivery process [9]. Order picking is one of the most labor intensive and expensive activity in every warehouse. Thus, automation of this task through the use driverless vehicles, such as, mobile picking robots, self-driving forklifts, autonomous inventory robots or unmanned aerial vehicles [10] are an attractive solution. The vehicle movement inside the warehouse lays on indoor localization and indoor navigation techniques based on WiFi communication technology [11][12].

We propose a communication system operating in the visible range using four ultra-bright white RGB and photodetector device based on two stacked multilayered a-SiC:H/a-Si:H structures that act as optical filters in the visible range [13][14]. The system is designed to establish bidirectional communication between a static infrastructure and an AGV.

The LEDs enable four transmission optical channels supplied by the modulation of the internal red and blue chips of the white RGB LED [15][16]. The propagation model of the channel is analyzed to characterize the signal coverage.

The possibility of tuning the spectral device sensitivity is analyzed and discussed using several optical bias conditions that induce different modulations of the electrical field along both front and back heterostructures, amplifying or cutting specific wavelengths [17]. This enables the identification of the transmitted individual input channels allows the location identification of the photodetector. The correct assignment of the identified signal to the location is the basis of the position algorithm proposed in this work .

A decoding strategy based on the evaluation of the output photocurrent for the detection of different optical signals is presented and discussed [18][19].

The rest of this paper is organized as follows. Section II describes the transmitter characterization. Section III describes the use of the receiver unit and the decoding strategy. Section IV addresses results and discussion. Section V goes into conclusions and presents guidelines for future work

## II. TRANSMITTER UNIT

The proposed VLC system intends to establish bidirectional infrastructure-to-device communication in an industrial indoor space. The proposed application is an automated warehouse where AGV pick goods from the racks and carry them to the packaging station where they are labeled and shipped.

The LED lamps placed at the warehouse ceiling are used to illuminate the space, to transmit information that enable position and navigation services and to transmit instructions to the AGV. The AVG robots communicate with the ceiling lamps to transmit information on the items that are being removed, which enables the update of the database.

The proposed system is composed of transmitter and the receiver modules, located at the LED lamps at the ceiling and at the AVG. Downlink communication is established from the ceiling lamps to the AVGs and uplink communication from the AVG to the correspondent ceiling lamp. The optical source of the transmitter at the ceiling lamps is composed of four white RGB LEDs. At the AGV the optical source is single-color LEDs.

The configuration proposed for the LED ceiling lamp includes four white RGB LED placed at the corners of a square (Figure 1a)). Here the red emitter of LEDs A and D and the blue emitters of LED B and C are used for data transmission. Assuming a quasi-circular signal distribution from each LED, the predicted signal coverage of this setup is shown in Figure 1b).

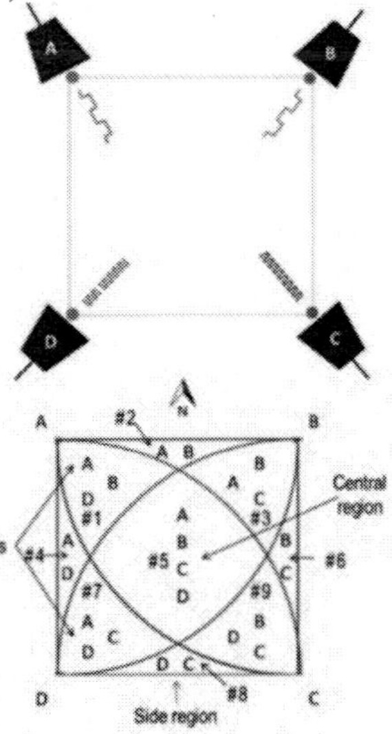


Figure 1. Configuration of the white LED lamp: a) modulated emitter of each LED ; b) signal coverage of the lamp.

It was assumed that each LED light contribution would overlap in the central region. In the lateral and corner parts this intersection would be partial due to the radiation patterns superposition of the closest two or three LEDs. The identification of the different signals is crucial for the identification of the position and thus for the indoor navigation.

The used RGB LEDs are commercial LEDs designed for general illumination providing therefore, high output power (550 mcd, 850 mcd and 320 mcd, for the red, green and blue emitters, respectively) and wide viewing angle. Analysis of the output light spectrum demonstrates the presence of three distinct gaussian peaks located in the blue (460 nm – 480 nm), green (520 nm – 540 nm) and red (619 nm – 624 nm) regions.

The light emitted by the LEDs is attenuated by the path distance to the receiver following the inverse of the square distance. Dependence on the wavelength is also stated using the propagation models (Friis equation).In Figure 2 it is shown the attenuation of the light signal dependence on the light wavelength for different distances between emitter and receiver units.

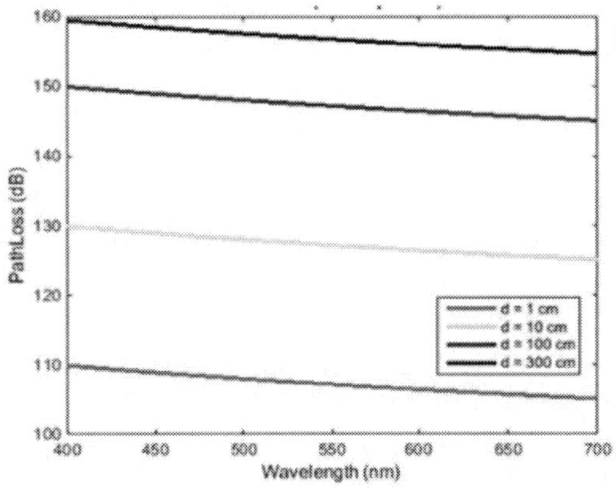


Figure 2. Attenuation of the light signal dependence on the light wavelength for different distances between emitter and receiver units sub-sections

The dependence on the wavelength is almost negligible, as the analyzed range (visible range) is very narrow. However, the dependence on the emitter-receiver distance is more evident, being very reduced at short distances and enlarging with wider distances.

## III. RECEIVER UNIT

The receiver module includes a photodetector to transform the light signal into an electric signal that is later demodulated and decoded to extract the transmitted information. The photodetector used for the transduction of the optical signal is a monolithic heterojunction composed of two pin structures based on a-Si:H and a-SiC:H and built on a glass substrate between two transparent electrical contacts (Figure 3).

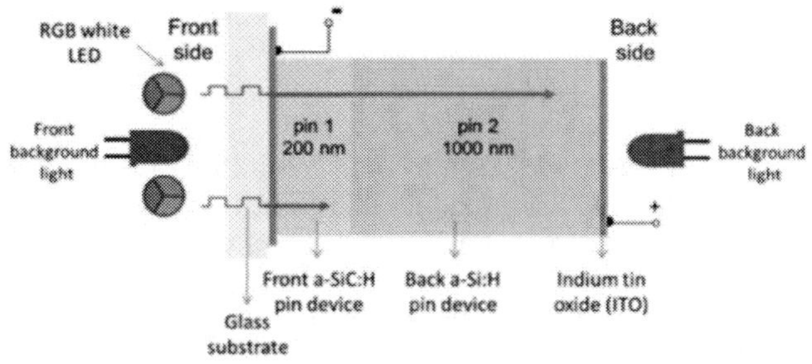


Figure 3. Simplified cross-section view of the photodetector.

The front pin a-SiC:H photodiode is responsible for the device sensitivity in the short wavelengths of the visible range (400 – 550 nm) due to its minor thickness (200 nm) and higher bandgap (2.1 eV). The back pin a-Si:H structure works in the complimentary past of the visible range, collecting the long wavelengths (520 nm – 700 nm). Selective absorption of long and short wavelengths can be achieved by adding steady state illumination of short wavelength (400 nm) to the photodetector. In Figure 4 it is displayed the output characteristics of the photodetector in transient mode measured without and under background light from both front and back sides.

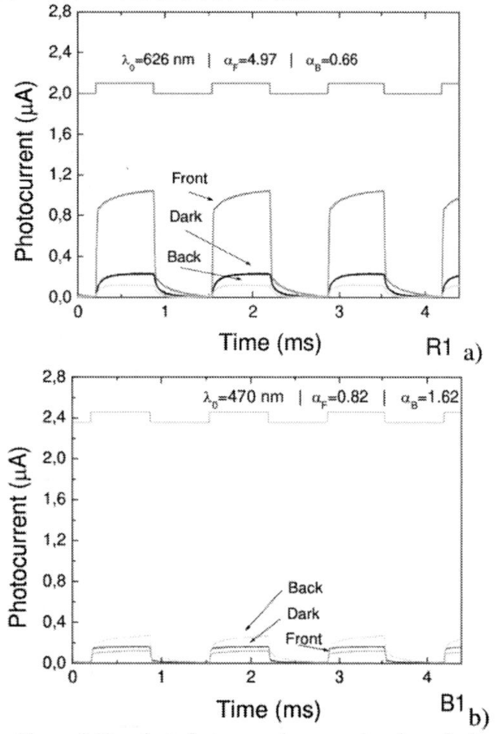


Figure 4. Transient photocurrent measured under pulsed illumination of the a) red and b) blue chips without optical bias and under front and back optical bias.

When this background light soaks the device, from the side of the a-SiC:H pin structure (front illumination), long wavelengths (red and green) provide amplification of the photocurrent, while short wavelengths (blue) attenuate the signal. Under background illumination, from the side of the a-Si:H pin structure (back illumination), the behavior is reversed. Signal amplification is obtained for shorter wavelengths and attenuation for longer wavelengths.

## IV. Results and Discussion

The frame used to transmit information related to the position and instructions to the AGV are coded in a word with a predefined size. The first and last blocks of the frame are used to ensure synchronism between the emitter and the receptor for correct demodulation of the transmitted signal. The second block is a word of 12 bits. In the fast and slow red and/or blue emitters, this word contains the information on the position within the navigation cell, which is assigned to the frequency. Slow emitters have a frequency half of the fast emitters. The green emitter is used to carry the identification of the unit cell. Its format was designed to ensure safe decode of the signals and prevent errors. It is a 12 bits word where the logic state of each bit never changes simultaneously with the other fast and slow red and blue emitters. The format of the word code is 0XXXX00YYYY0, where XXXX addresses the line and YYYY the column of the unit navigation cell. The third block of every emitter is a 12 bits word, reserved for the transmission of the information related to the available racks inside each navigation area. As the area covered by the navigation unit comprises nine cardinal sub-sections containing four quadrants each, it is necessary 9 x 4 = 36 bits to infer which of these spatial positions, i.e. racks, are available. Each of the channels (12 bits available) transmits information about 3 sub-sections, using 4 bits for each. The first bit is assigned to the first quadrant, the second to the second quadrant and so on. Slow emitters of each navigation cell transmit information about northwest, north and northeast directions, fast emitters at the bottom about southwest, south and southeast, and the green emitters about west, center and east positions.

When the AGV reaches the desired position defined by the route, it removes the rack and carries it to the packaging station. At the same time it provides information on this task, that is necessary for database update using the uplink channel. The establishment of this communication link demands the identification of both partners (lamp and robot). The uplink channel uses three wavelengths and the info is coded in a 3x32 bits word with a simple structure of four blocks: two synchronization blocks (2x4 bits) located at the beginning and at the end of the word and two informative blocks (2x12 bits) in the middle. The first 12 bits block contains the identification of the ceiling luminaire that is illuminating the AGV and the identification of the AGV responsible for picking the items from the rack.

The test case used to validate the proposed communication scheme is displayed in Figure 5, that shows the specific blocks of the 32 bits word of each emitter assigned to the lamps and to the mobile robot.

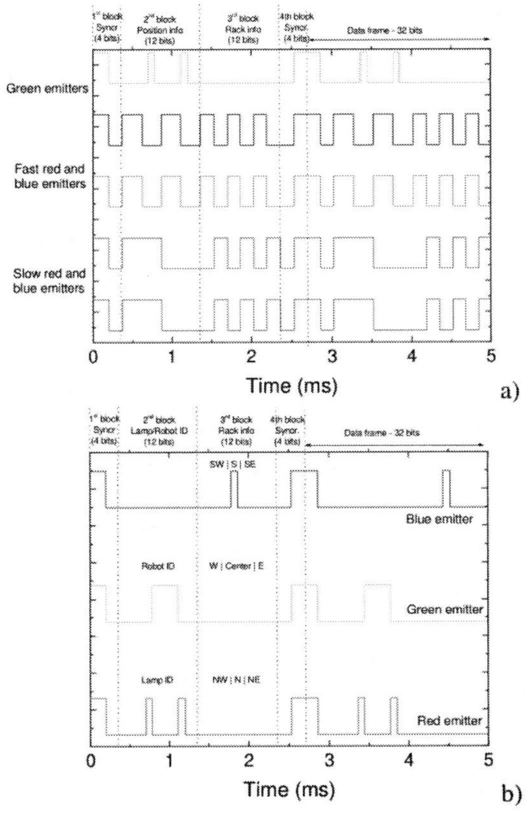


Figure 5. Codification of the optical signals transmitted by the: a) ceiling lamp; b) mobile picking robot.

In the code transmitted by the ceiling lamp (Figure 5a), the green transmitters send the code 1100 | 000010000100 | 0000 0000 0000 | 0011, which corresponds to the navigation cell with identification 1-2 (line 1: 0001, column 2: 0010) and to the information that there is no rack placed in the position west, center and east of the same cell. Slow emitters transmit the 1100 | 111111000000 | 0011 0011 0011 | 0011 code which identifies them as top emitters inside the navigation unit cell and states that in northwest, north and northeast sub-sections the third and fourth quadrants contain available racks that can be picked by the robot. In these quadrants, the 1st and 2nd quadrants are empty of available racks. Fast emitters transmit the code 1100 | 111000111000 | 1100 1100 1100 | 0011 which represents their position as bottom emitters in the navigation unit cell and informs that in the southwest, south and southeast sub-sections the 1st and 2nd quadrants contain available racks to be moved while the 3rd and 4th racks are not accessible as they are empty

In Figure 6, it is displayed the photocurrent signal measured by the mobile robot under variable conditions of optical bias (without and with front/back steady state background light). The signal was acquired in position (9) of the navigation cell 1-2, when the picking robot moves in the forward lane to remove a rack of the first quadrant of sub-section southwest (SE).

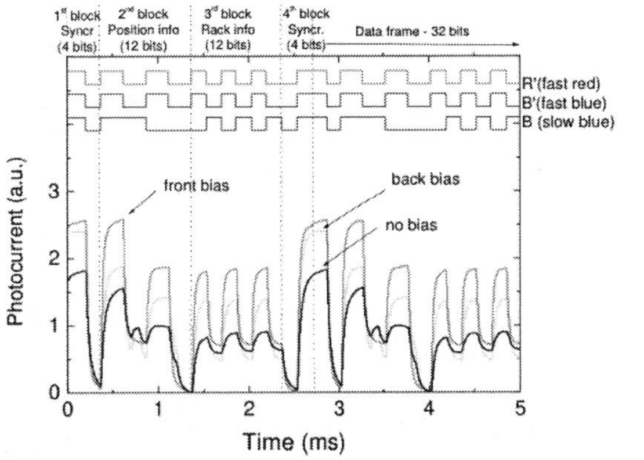


Figure 6. Photocurrent signal (measured without and with front/back steady state light) measured at position (9) of the navigation cell 1-2 after removing the contribution from the green emitters At the top it is displayed the optical signal of each emitter.

The signal was acquired in the central position (9) of the navigation cell 1-2, when the picking robot moves in the forward lane to remove a rack of the first quadrant of sub-section southwest (SE). At this position the optical excitation comes from the fast red and blue emitters and from the slow blue emitter. The displayed output signal has already been removed of the contribution due to the green optical excitation. In the graph, the trigger event allows easy synchronization and identification of each transmitted frame. This is noticeable by the highest peaks of the front photocurrent signal (represented in the graphs by the magenta line), as well as by the idle bits (all emitters are set to 1). This combination results in photocurrent amplification when the device is soaked by front steady state illumination. By opposition, the same signal under back background light is decreased.

Then, it is necessary to decode the next blocks of the data frame. It is assumed that in the front photocurrent the highest levels correspond to the presence of the red light, while the lowest ones to its absence, which allows the immediate recognition of the ON-OFF states for the red channel. The same reasoning can be used to analyze the back-photocurrent signal. Here the highest levels are assigned to the presence of the blue input signal and the lowest levels to its nonexistence, which allows the decoding of the blue channel. However, at the regions where there are two different signals transmitted by the same wavelength, this approach is not feasible, as it is necessary to infer which of these is channels is on or off. The approach used to decode each optical state was based on the use of a calibration curve. This was obtained by scaling all the possible signal output levels (Figure 7, solid black line) and measuring the photocurrent signal under front optical bias using two red and two blue optical signals. The driving current of each LED emitter was adjusted to provide different levels of photo excitation. On the right side of the picture in Figure 7, it is shown the label of the modulated emitters that correspond to each photocurrent level.

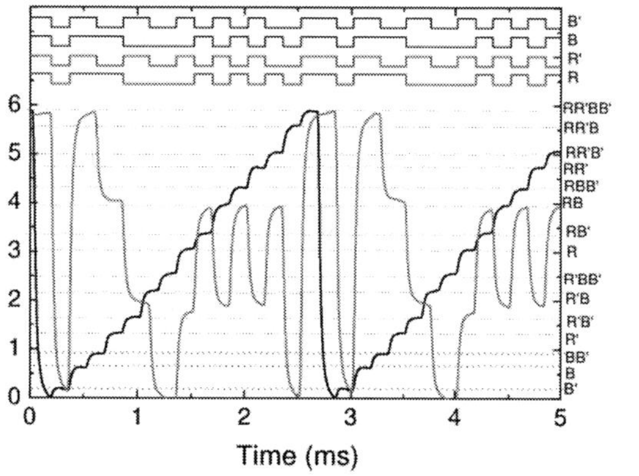


Figure 7. Front photocurrent signal measured along the forward path at the central position of the navigation cell. In superposition it is displayed the calibration grid.

In Figure 8, it is displayed the front photocurrent signal due to the optical signal transmitted by the AGV after concluding a specific task of items removal.

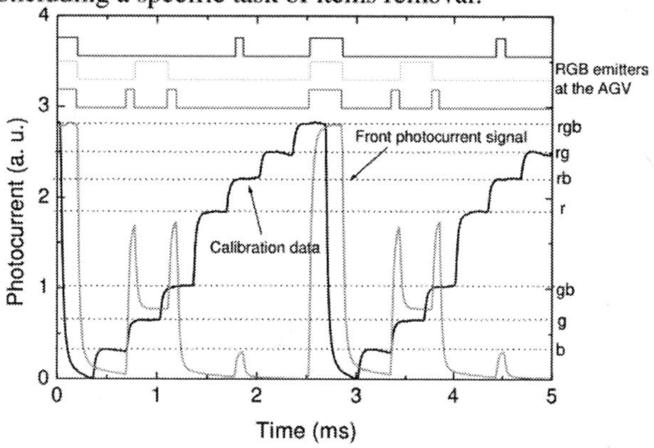


Figure 8. Front photocurrent signal transmitted by the robot when removing a rack. In superposition it is placed the calibration curve with 8 levels.

The calibration curve obtained with the 8 possible combinations is also displayed for decoding purposes.

## V. CONCLUSION AND FUTURE WORKS

Simultaneous navigation and data transmission based on visible light communication were presented using bidirectional communication based on VLC between the infrastructure and AGV in an industrial application of an automated warehouse. The infrastructure is the ceiling LED lamp and the AVG a mobile warehouse picking robot. The transmitted data is encoded in a 32 bits word, defined using specific data frames in each communication channel. Codification of the optical signals ensured synchronization between frames and was also designed to make the decoding process more robust and prevent errors that might provide wrong identification of the correspondent spatial position.

Future work includes a more complete characterization of the channel gain and integration of the propagation model with the specific amplification features of the device under light bias.

## ACKNOWLEDGMENT

This work was sponsored by FCT – Fundação para a Ciência e a Tecnologia, within the Research Unit CTS – Center of Technology and systems, reference UIDB/00066/2020 and by IPL/2020/Geo-Loc_ISEL.

## REFERENCES

[1] K. Panta and J. Armstrong, “Indoor localisation using white LEDs”, Electron. Lett. 48 (4), pp. 228–230, 2012.

[2] A. Jovicic, J. Li, and T. Richardson, “Visible light communication: opportunities, challenges and the path to market”. J IEEE Communications Magazine, 51, pp. 26-32, 2013.

[3] W. Zhang and M. Kavehrad, “A 2-D indoor localization system based on visible light LED,” in Proc. IEEE Photonics Society Summer Topical Conf.—Optical Wireless Systems Applications, pp. 80–81, 2012.

[4] W. Zhang, M. I. S. Chowdhury, and M. Kavehrad, “Asynchronous indoor positioning system based on visible light communications”, Optical Eng. 53(4), pp. 045105, 2014.

[5] A. Jovicic, J. Li, and T. Richardson, “Visible light communication: opportunities, challenges and the path to market,” Communic. Mag. IEEE, 51,12, pp. 26–32, 2013.

[6] T. Tanaka and S. Haruyama, “New position detection method using image sensor and visible light leds,” in Machine Vision, ICMV’09. 2nd Int. Conf. IEEE, 2009, pp. 150–153, 2009.

[7] T. Komiyama, K. Kobayashi, K. Watanabe, T. Ohkubo, and Y. Kurihara, “Demonstration of Visible light Text data transmission system using LED lamp”, Proceedings of SICE Annual Conference, IEEE, pp. 1926–1928, 2011.

[8] W. Ding, “Study of Smart Warehouse Management System Based on the IOT”. In: Du Z. (eds) Intelligence Computation and Evolutionary Computation. Advances in Intelligent Systems and Computing, vol 180. Springer, Berlin, Heidelberg, 2013.

[9] R. Koster, T. Duc, and K. Roodbergen, “Design and control of warehouse order picking: A literature review”, European Journal of Operational Research, 182 (16), pp. 481-501, 2007.

[10] J. Gu, M. Goetschalckx, and L. McGinnis “Research on warehouse operation: A comprehensive review”, European Journal of Operational Research, 177 (1), pp. 1-21, 2007.

[11] P. R. Wurman, R. D’Andrea, and M. Mountz, “Coordinating Hundreds of Cooperative, Autonomous Vehicles in Warehouses”, AI Magazine, 29 (1), pp. 9 – 20., 2008.

[12] Z. Xiaoguang and L. Wei, “The research of network architecture in warehouse management system based on RFID and WSN integration”, 2008 IEEE International Conference on Automation and Logistics, Qingdao, pp. 2556-2560, 2008..

[13] P. Louro, M. Vieira, M. A. Vieira, S. Amaral, J. Costa, M. Fernandes, Sensors & Actuators: A Physical. 172 (1), pp. 35-39, 2011.

[14] M. Vieira, A. Fantoni, M. Fernandes, P. Louro, G. Lavareda, C.N. Carvalho, J. Nanosc. and Nanotech. 9 (7), pp. 4022-4027, 2009.

[15] P. Louro, V. Silva; J. Costa; M. A. Vieira, and M. Vieira, "Added transmission capacity in VLC systems using white RGB based LEDs and WDM devices ", Proc. SPIE 9899, Optical Sensing and Detection IV, 98990F, 2016.

[16] M. A. Vieira, M. Vieira, V. Silva, and P. Louro, "Optical signal processing for indoor positioning using a-SiC:H technology" Proc. SPIE 9891, Silicon Photonics and Photonic Integrated Circuits V, 98911Z, 2016.

[17] M. Vieira, P. Louro, M. A. Vieira, M. Fernandes, J. Costa, A. Fantoni, and M. A. Barata, "Optical processing devices based on a-SiC:H multilayer architectures", Phys. Status Solidi C 7, No. 3–4, pp. 1184– 1187, 2010.

[18] P. Louro, M. Vieira, and M. A. Vieira, "Coding schemes in a communication system based on visible-light communication", Proc. SPIE 10947, Next-Generation Optical Communication: Components, Sub-Systems, and Systems VIII, 109470G, 2019.

[19] P. Louro, J. Costa, M. Vieira, and M. A. Vieira, Y. Vygranenko, "Use of VLC for indoors navigation with RGB LEDs and a-SiC:H photodetector", Proc. of SPIE, vol 10231, Optical sensors 2017

# Modular Wi-Fi Sensor Node for Indoor Environmental Sensing Applications

Philipp Bolte
*Dept. of Electronics and Circuit Technology*
*South Westphalia University of Applied Sciences*
Soest, Germany
e-mail: bolte.philipp@fh-swf.de

Ulf Witkowski
*Dept. of Electronics and Circuit Technology*
*South Westphalia University of Applied Sciences*
Soest, Germany
e-mail: witkowski.ulf@fh-swf.de

***Abstract*—A wireless sensor node with Wi-Fi interface has been developed and applied to measure air quality parameters. The node can be used for different indoor sensing applications, but the currently addressed application context is to reduce the risk of virus infection that is related to the aerosol concentration in a room. As a helpful measure, the carbon dioxide (CO2) concentration can be considered because there is a relation between CO2 concentration and aerosol concentration. Two different approaches of CO2 measurements, direct and indirect, are tested. Captured data is wirelessly transmitted via Wi-Fi to a database for detailed analysis. By using multiple sensor nodes, a spatial distribution of CO2 can be calculated by using the inverse distance weighting interpolation technique. The resulting CO2 distribution data can be used to optimize the number of required sensor nodes for a specific room and their placements. Another aspect is the dynamics of the CO2 concentration when ventilating the room, e.g., by opening windows to reduce the aerosol concentration in a room. A single sensor node or multiple nodes can be used to set up an alarm system that indicates pending room ventilation in case of high CO2 concentration. A set of five sensor nodes have been installed into a small room to record CO2 concentration over time with a closed window and when airing the room.**

***Keywords-Wireless sensor; Distributed sensing; CO2 concentration measurement; Aerosol distribution***

## I. Introduction

Virus diseases like the pandemic Covid-19 require multiple approaches to reduce the number of infections. One approach is to filter infectious particles by optimized filter systems in indoor scenarios but these systems can be difficult and expensive to install. Another approach is to apply regular room ventilation to reduce virus concentration. To optimize this process, a measure can be helpful to identify the virus concentration. For Covid-19 there is an expected relation between virus concentration of SARS-CoV-2 in the air and the aerosol concentration because viruses are usually connected to aerosols emitted during human's breathing and speech. But to directly measure the aerosol concentration is difficult. It is much simpler to measure the carbon dioxide (CO2) concentrations instead because current research has shown a correlation between aerosol and CO2 concentrations [1]. Retrofitting existing buildings with modern Heating, Ventilation and Air Conditioning (HVAC) systems incorporating automatic ventilation is a challenging task [2]. The extensive use of CO2 sensors in classrooms and offices without automatic HVAC systems could improve the ventilation habits and therefore reduce the CO2 concentration and consequently the concentration of potentially virus-contaminated aerosols. CO2 sensors and related measurement systems can be easily deployed in indoor scenarios. But it is usually necessary to install more than a single sensor at different positions in a room to get a realistic view of the CO2 concentration and distribution in order to optimize ventilation frequency and duration.

We propose a modular Sensor Node (SN) that enables the deployment for different scenarios. The SN is built around the self-designed IoTyze Wi-Fi module. A Nondispersive Infrared (NDIR) CO2 and a Volatile Organic Compounds (VOC) sensor can be connected to the SN. The gathered data from the connected sensors is buffered and transmitted via the Message Queuing Telemetry Transport (MQTT) protocol using a Wi-Fi modem every 30 seconds. One use case is the local display of the measured air quality parameters to support the regular airing of the room. A display is connected to show the air quality parameters. An optical and acoustical alert is triggered if the air quality parameters reach a critical limit to indicate the need for ventilation. The measured data is stored in a database as evidence.

For a second application, a network of multiple SN is deployed to measure the indoor spatial CO2 concentration. The spatial CO2 concentration in classrooms is not uniformly distributed, it depends on room geometry as well as on the type of ventilation [3]. Experiments have shown that the CO2 concentration in occupied space can be estimated using computational fluid dynamics (CFD) simulation if the boundary conditions are known [5]. The concept was only applied to simple room geometries. A network of multiple SN could be used to experimentally determine the optimal location for a single CO2 sensor inside complex structured rooms (e.g., classrooms with many tables and chairs) without the need for complex CFD simulations. This paper proposes a method for interpolating the CO2 concentration measurements that is tested with preliminary data recorded in home office.

The paper is organized as follows: In Section 2 the architecture of the developed sensor node is described. This includes hardware components, integrated sensors for CO2 measurement, and the data flow for storing the sensor data in a database. The interfaces to access the sensor data locally or remote via online display are introduced in Section 3. Also comparisons are made for direct and indirect measurement of CO2 concentration. Data analysis and spatial interpolation is explained in Section 4. Section 5 concludes the paper.

## II. Sensor Node Architecture

We propose the use of the IoTyze Wi-Fi board as the main controller for the SN. This board combines a powerful STM32 Microcontroller (MCU), an ESP32 Wi-Fi System on Chip (SoC) and additional periphery, as shown in Figure 1. One of the sensors or both, i.e., SCD30 and BME680, can be connected to the board. The display unit is an optional feature if a local display is required. The IoTyze ecosystem provides a software framework with a variety of different sensor drivers and an easy-to-use file-based device configuration via USB flash-drive emulation [4]. The use of a Wi-Fi modem supports high transmission rates but requires an external power supply. The LoRaWAN and LTE NB-IoT variants are not used because of the limited bandwidth. A battery-supplied operation is not considered because of the high current consumption of the used sensors due to continuous measurements. The use of a USB power supply for the sensor nodes is not a problem anyway since the SNs are placed indoor at a fixed position.

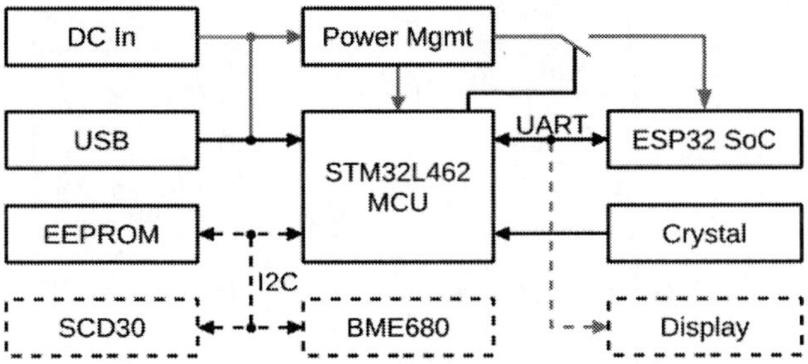


Fig. 1. Hardware block diagram of the sensor node

### A. Hardware

The IoTyze Wi-Fi board integrates an STM32L462 host processor and an ESP32 SoC that executes the TCP/IP stack. The communication between the host processor and the Wi-Fi module is established using UART with a baud rate of 115200 bit/s. External oscillators are connected to the host processor to provide precise timing. An I²C EEPROM is used for storing the device configuration and status data. A micro USB port is used to access the device configuration and for the power supply. The board can also be supplied by using a DC connector. The power rails, GPIOs, UART-, I²C- and SPI-interfaces from the host processor are available through a 20 pin header. The sensors, including the optional display, are connected to the controller board using this connector.

### B. Air Quality Sensors

The main sensor device to estimate the aerosol concentration is the Sensirion SCD30 sensor to measure the CO2 concentration because of the correlation between CO2 concentration and aerosols. Furthermore, this sensor also measures temperature and humidity. The device is connected to the host processor using the I²C bus. The measurement of the CO2 concentration is based on NDIR principles. The sample gas is irradiated by a wideband light source and two photosensors with specific passbands that measure the difference of a wavelength of 4.3 um, that is attenuated by CO2 molecules, compared to a wavelength of 4 um, that is minimally absorbed by air gases [6]. CO2 concentrations between 0 parts per million (ppm) and 40000 ppm can be measured and the accuracy is specified by 30 ppm or 3% [7]. The direct measurement of CO2 concentration with an NDIR sensor is fairly expensive.

Furthermore, the SN can be equipped with a Bosch BME680 VOC sensor. This sensor integrates four different sensing principles for gas, humidity, pressure and temperature. It has been optimized for IoT, home automation and control and other applications. The VOC sensing is based on proven sensing principles, i.e., depending on the type of gas that is flowing along a heated metal-oxide surface different resulting conductivities could be electrically measured [8]. A survey of students has shown that the indoor comfort satisfaction of students does not exclusively depend on CO2 concentration and that other micro-climate factors (e.g., temperature, humidity, smell) must also be taken into account [9]. The hotplate sensors measure a wider range of VOC pollutants, e.g., outgassing from garbage, paint and furniture that is processed by the integrated Bosch BSEC sensor fusion which outputs the CO2 equivalent based on the correlation of VOC and CO2 concentrations in humans exhaled breath [10]. The data from the sensor fusion of the BME680 measurements can be used as additional air quality parameters.

### C. Data Flow

The proposed SN reads data from the connected sensors and performs the required data preprocessing for transmission of the buffered measurements as shown in Figure 2.

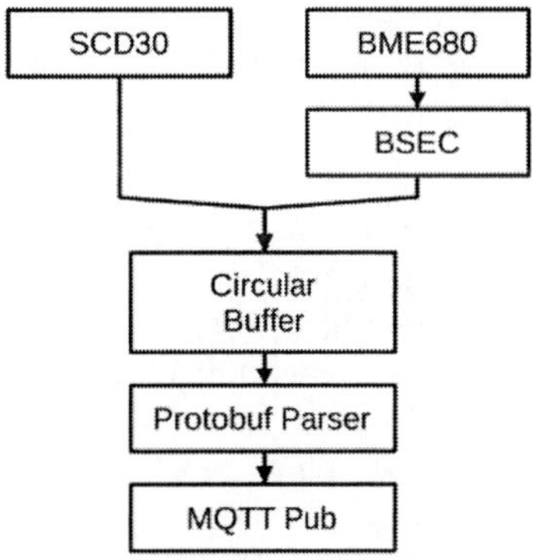


Fig. 2. Internal data flow of the sensor node

The CO2 concentration, temperature and humidity readings from the SCD30 sensor with a sampling period of 2 seconds are directly transferred into a circular FIFO buffer. The data from the BME680 is processed by the proprietary Bosch Sensortec Environmental Cluster (BSEC) sensor fusion library [11]. The BSEC sensor fusion outputs virtual sensor values for temperature, humidity, ambient pressure, Indoor Air Quality (IAQ) and CO2 equivalent with a sampling period of 3 seconds that is stored in the circular FIFO buffer. The circular FIFO buffer is implemented around a nested C structure that is generated by the Nanopb compiler from a payload description [12]. The FIFO buffer is converted into the binary protocol buffers data format using the Nanopb encoder. The binary payload is transferred by a publish message using the MQTT protocol. For the proposed sample application, the payload is decoded and stored into an InfluxDB database by a Node-RED instance. The data can be exported to a CSV formatted text file for further processing and analysis.

## III. AIR QUALITY DISPLAY

For the first application, the SN was equipped with a display and a buzzer, as shown in Figure 3. The hardware is placed inside a 3D printed case. The sensors are located at the back of the case. An air-permeable cap is used as mechanical protection. The device is supplied by an external 5V power supply with a standard micro USB connector. The software was developed for use with both, the SCD30 CO2 and the BME680 VOC sensor, but also works with one of the sensors, lacking the values of the disconnected device.

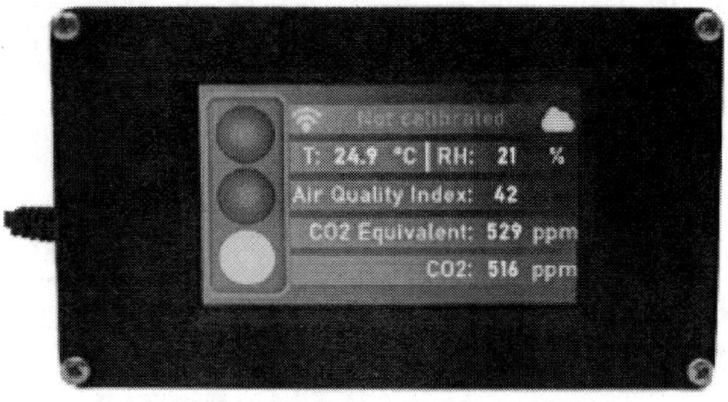


Fig. 3. Fully equipped sensor node

### A. Local Display

The measured environmental parameters from the SCD30 sensor and the BSEC sensor fusion are additionally fed into an air quality state management software module. This module classifies the air quality based on the last CO2 reading, the IAQ estimation and the assessments of the standard DIN EN 13779 [13]. The standard refers to CO2 concentrations above the ambient level for classification. The globally averaged CO2 concentration for the year 2019 was 410.5 ppm [14]. For simplicity, an ambient CO2 concentration of 400 ppm was assumed. High air quality is assumed if both CO2 readings were below 950 ppm. For concentrations between 950 ppm and 1200 ppm air quality is considered sufficient. High pollution with an immediate need for ventilation is assumed if the CO2 concentration exceeds 1200 ppm. The higher CO2 reading is used for classification if both sensors are connected.

The current temperature, humidity, IAQ, CO2 (SCD30), CO2 equivalent (BSEC) and the overall air quality assessment are shown on a 4.3" TFT display, as shown in Figure 3. An acoustic alert is triggered if the air quality exceeds a critical limit. The local display should motivate the people to periodically air the room. That way, the CO2 concentration and thus also the expose of potentially infectious aerosols can be kept below a critical level.

### B. Online Display

The buffered sensor data is transmitted to an MQTT broker using the ESP32 Wi-Fi modem every 30 seconds. For the air quality display application, the data is stored in an InfluxDB time-series database [16]. The stored data sets can be displayed on a web dashboard using Grafana [17]. The actual CO2 measurements and the CO2 equivalent estimations from the VOC measurements over a period of 4 days are shown in Figure 4.

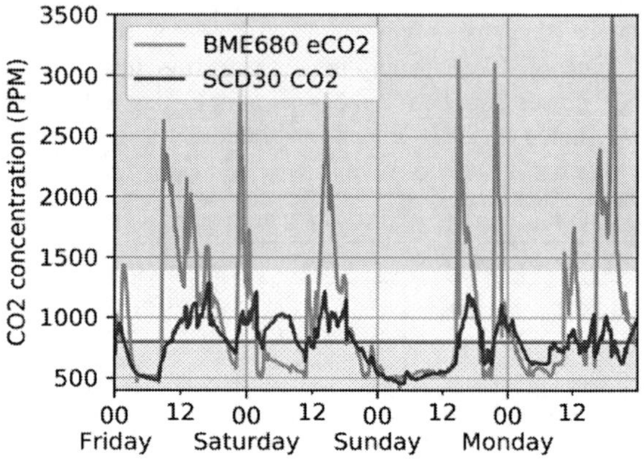


Fig. 4. Recorded actual (SCD30) and VOC based estimated (BME680) CO2 concentration

In the event of a revealed Covid infection, the recorded data is possibly useful for a more accurate risk assessment to prevent a further spread of the virus.

### C. CO2 equivalent estimation

The NDIR CO2 sensors are significantly more expensive compared to the VOC sensors. The estimated CO2 equivalent from the BSEC sensor fusion is based on the assumption of the presence of human breath only. For other sources of CO2, the estimation will usually be too small, as shown in Figure 4 for the time between Saturday midnight and noon. The gas resistance measurement is sensitive to a wide range of VOCs. Outgassing from furniture [18], detergents [19] or personal care products [22] results in a higher total VOC concentration, causing too high CO2 estimates. The spikes for the CO2 estimations in Figure 4 likely result from such effects. The cheap VOC sensor is therefore not capable of replacing the actual NDIR sensor if accurate CO2 concentration values are required. For the use in an air quality display, the sensor could be suitable nevertheless because the readings determined are usually too high if other VOC pollutants are present. In this case, the airing of the room would be recommended anyway. Especially, if a larger number of sensors nodes should be deployed in large buildings to support air purity and ventilation, a significant price advantage of the BME680 becomes obvious.

## IV. Spatial CO2 concentration

Objective of the proposed SN is the reduction of aerosol concentration indoors by indicating high CO2 concentrations. In case of detection of high CO2 concentration, room ventilation should be performed for a specific time. But the structure of a room and the localisation of windows and doors affect the aerosol distribution [21] and therefore the efficiency of ventilation in terms of local reduction of aerosol concentrations. As solution, multiple sensor nodes can be deployed to measure the CO2 concentration at different locations inside a room. The use of multiple SNs helps to measure aerosol concentration in badly ventilated room corners and regions away from a window to optimize the ventilation frequency and duration and therefore to lower the aerosol concentration in all parts of a room. Theoretically, it is also possible to estimate the indoor aerosol distribution by mathematically modeling [20], but this is too complex for the proposed application, especially when equipping several rooms with sensor nodes. As experimental approach, multiple sensor nodes have been placed at different locations inside a room to get the spatial CO2 concentration. The measured data was used to visualize and evaluate the air exchange during ventilation in order to optimize the ventilation process. This set-up could further be used to determine the optimal location for a single air quality display in typical room structures.

### A. Experimental Setup

Due to the current Covid situation, it was not possible to perform measurements under realistic conditions with many humans being in a room like a university lecture hall. Therefore, preliminary data was recorded in the home office with a limited area of 19 m². The layout of the room is shown in Figure 5. SN *1* is placed on a TV rack in front of the room. SN 2 is placed on the upper side of the desk near a window. SN *3* is located in the opposite direction of the desk. SN *4* is mounted in a nested corner of the room. SN *5* is located near the door. All sensors are placed at a height of 1.5 m to limit the interpolation to 2 dimensions. The experiment begins with the door and all windows closed in order to demonstrate the effect of ventilation.

The time between the shown measurements was determined experimental in a way to best demonstrate the effect of airing and the rise of CO2 concentration after closing the window. First measurements of CO2 concentrations are performed just before the door and window *a* are opened. After 30 seconds the next measurements are taken. The door and the window are closed after 5 minutes of open time and a last set of measurements are acquired after additional 5 minutes.

### B. Interpolation

The measured CO2 concentrations are interpolated on a plane, representing a cross-section of the room. One challenge of the spatial interpolation for this application is the limited number of supporting points. The few measurement locations are further not placed on a regular grid. Basic multivariant interpolation techniques, e.g., bilinear interpolation, rely on a

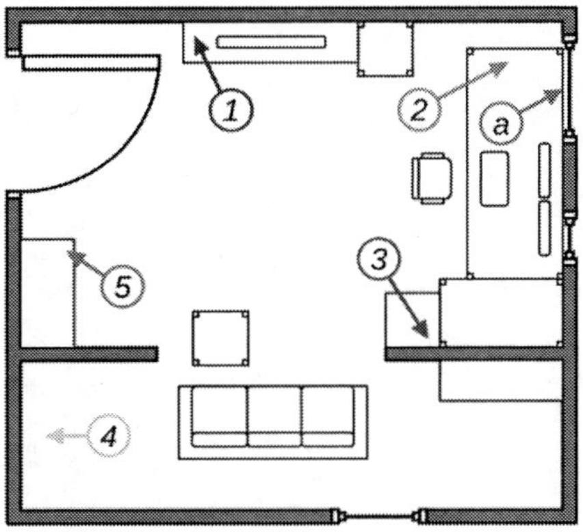


Fig. 5. Room layout with furniture, door, window (a) and position of 5 sensors

regular grid, which is why these methods are not suitable for this application [23]. Methods from geostatistics, e.g., kriging or inverse distance weighting (IDW) can be used with irregular distributed data. Kriging is a commonly used geostatistical approach assuming a spatial correlation between the sample points [24]. The data from the five SNs is not sufficient to create a meaningful variogram. Therefore, the deterministic IDW approach was used for interpolation. The estimated value is calculated by the values and distances to all sampled points, as shown in Equation 1 [25]. The weighting of each sample point only depends on the distance raised to the power of $\mu$, neglecting the unknown spatial correlation. The interpolation points can only take values between the minima and maxima of the support points.

$$F(x,y) = \begin{cases} \frac{\sum_{k=1}^{N}(\frac{1}{d_k})^{\mu} f_k}{\sum_{k=1}^{N}(\frac{1}{d_k})^{\mu}} & \text{if all } d_k \neq 0 \\ f_k & \text{if any } d_k = 0 \end{cases} \tag{1}$$

$F$ = Estimation for coordinate $x$, $y$
$N$ = Number of samples
$d_k$ = Distance between estimation and sample
$\mu$ = Power, determines the smoothing
$f_k$ = Sample value

### C. Results

Figure 6 shows the spatial CO2 concentration at a height of 1.5 m before the experiment is started. The CO2 concentration is almost identical at all measuring points (1416-1466 ppm) except for position *1* that is located near the door with 1239 ppm. Fresh air flowing through the gap underneath the door could explain the drop in CO2 concentration at this sampling point.

The measurements recorded 30 seconds after opening the door and window *a* are shown in Figure 7. Fresh air is flowing through window a in direction of the door. The CO2 concentration near the window is 468 ppm whereas in the corner of the room at position *4* still 1302 ppm is measured. Shortly after the start of airing, a concentration drop is visible

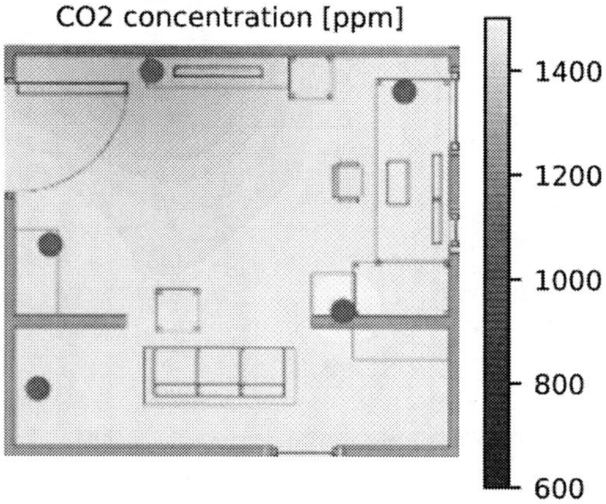


Fig. 6. Spatial CO2 concentration just before airing ($t = 0$)

in the direction of the window. The sensor readings measured at position *2* near the window are also fluctuating while the window is open. The airing results in a noticeable pulsating airflow near the window, causing a temporal variation of CO2 concentration near the window. Total airing time is 5 minutes.

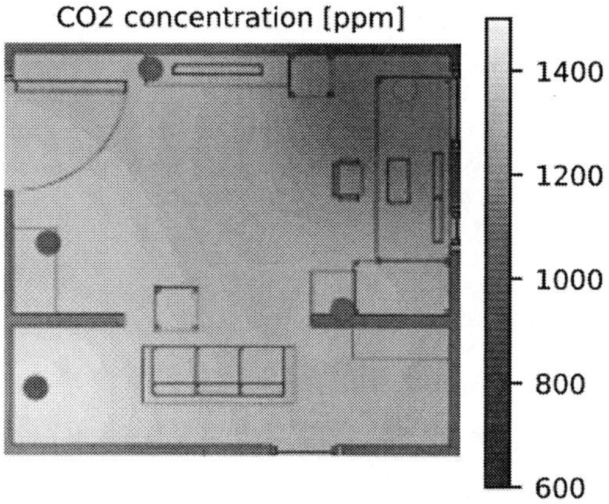


Fig. 7. Spatial CO2 concentration after ($t = 30\,\mathrm{s}$) seconds airing

The last measurements taken 5 minutes after the window *a* and the door were closed are shown in Figure 8. The CO2 concentration now settles between 664 ppm at position *1* near the door and 983 ppm at position *3* at the corner of the desk. The measurement at position *2* in the opposite direction of the desk near the window is 839 ppm. The CO2 concentration in the immediate environment of the workplace is already increasing after a short time when working at this place. To have an efficient result of the ventilation, i.e., low CO2 concentration in all regions of a room, multiple sensor nodes should be used to get a detailed view of the CO2 distribution.

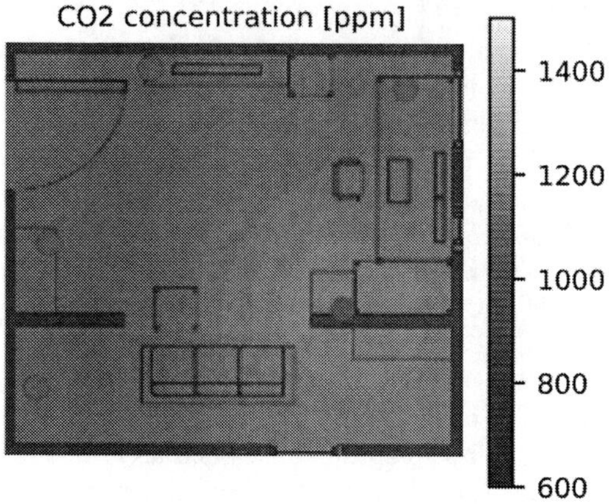


Fig. 8. Spatial CO2 concentration 5 minutes after the end of airing, i.e., at time $t = (5 + 5)\,\mathrm{min}$

Here, a simple guideline should be developed where to place the sensors in the room for typical room structures. In the proposed scenarios the sensors are wirelessly connected to a database. Future postprocessing of the recorded sensor data including visualization can be used to optimize number and position of sensors in a room. Result can be a guideline for e.g., facility managers to optimize SN deployment in different rooms and to reduce infection risk by keeping aerosol concentrations at reasonable low levels.

## V. CONCLUSIONS

The deployment of the proposed air quality sensor with local display and alert functionality supports the ventilation habits to keep the room CO2 concentration below a critical limit. The online data logging could serve as an indicator for the infection risk in case of a detected Covid infection. The estimated CO2 equivalent from the BSEC sensor fusion is not as accurate as the directly measured value from the NDIR sensor but it is still sufficient as a rough indicator of the air quality. The BME680 sensor could be used for a low-cost variant of the sensor node, as the values are estimated rather too high. Due to the cost-efficiency of the SN, multiple of these nodes can be used in a single room to get a good view of spatial CO2 concentration.

The spatial distribution of the CO2 concentration as well as its dynamic change has been recorded in small room during an airing period. Right at the beginning of the airing a concentration gradient originating from the window was observed. In the direct vicinity of the workplace, an increased CO2 concentration is already detected shortly after the airing was stopped. From the preliminary data it can be concluded that the well-elaborated location of a single CO2 sensor inside the room is highly relevant. The positioning near doors and windows is not recommended because of possible draught resulting in too low measurement values not representing high CO2 concentrations as they may remain in isolated or nested regions of a room. If it is not possible to use multiple sensors, a single sensor should be placed further inside the room close to the workplaces or in room corner with some distance to a window.

In future work, measurements have to be performed under real conditions in crowded lecture rooms and halls. Due to the current Covid restrictions, experiments under those conditions were not possible so far. It has to be analyzed how many sensor nodes should be used for typical room structures in order to have a cost-efficient but still safe solution to measure CO2 concentration as basis to start the ventilation process. A planning tool could be developed that automatically calculates the number and positioning of sensor nodes inside a room. Database for this approach is the recorded sensor data captured in the planning phase when for a set-up time more nodes than required are used in a room to get sufficient sensor data from different regions of a room. As part of this planning tool, the interpolation quality has to be analyzed. The adjusted inverse distance weighting (AIDW) interpolation could be used to account for shielding effects resulting from space-dividing elements [26]. Furthermore, the used IDW approach could be compared to other interpolation techniques (e.g., radial basis functions [27]) to determine the best fitting method for spatial distribution of CO2 in occupied space. The final planning tool can be an interactive graphical tool representing room structure and placement of sensors and optionally extended by dynamic sensor data visualization for analysis options.

## REFERENCES


[1] A. Hartmann and M. Kriegel, "Risk assessment of aerosols loaded with virus based on CO2-concentration," *Preprint*, Jul. 2020, doi: 10.14279/DEPOSITONCE-10362.3.

[2] Z. Ma, P. Cooper, D. Daly, and L. Ledo, "Existing building retrofits: Methodology and state-of-the-art," *Energy and Buildings*, vol. 55, pp. 889–902, Dec. 2012, doi: 10.1016/j.enbuild.2012.08.018.

[3] N. Mahyuddin, H. B. Awbi, and M. Alshitawi, "The spatial distribution of carbon dioxide in rooms with particular application to classrooms," *Indoor and Built Environment*, vol. 23, no. 3, pp. 433–448, May 2014, doi: 10.1177/1420326X13512142.

[4] P. Bolte, U. Witkowski, and R. Morgenstern, "Open Lorawan Sensor Node Architecture for Agriculture Applications," *3rd International Conference on Internet of Things (CIoT 2021)*, Sept. 2021, Canada, accepted for publication.

[5] A. Bulińska, Z. Popiolek, and Z. Buliński, "Experimentally validated CFD analysis on sampling region determination of average indoor carbon dioxide concentration in occupied space," *Building and Environment*, vol. 72, pp. 319–331, Feb. 2014, doi: 10.1016/j.buildenv.2013.11.001.

[6] J. Hodgkinson, R. Smith, W. O. Ho, J. R. Saffell, and R. P. Tatam, "Non-dispersive infra-red (NDIR) measurement of carbon dioxide at 4.2 μm in a compact and optically efficient sensor," *Sensors and Actuators B: Chemical*, vol. 186, pp. 580–588, Sep. 2013, doi: 10.1016/j.snb.2013.06.006.

[7] Sensirion, "CO2, humidity, and temperature sensor," SCD30 datasheet, Rev. 1.0, May 2020. Accessed Jun. 08, 2021. [Online]. Available: https://www.sensirion.com/de/download-center/kohlendioxidsensoren-co2/co2-sensor.

[8] T. Lin, X. Lv, Z. Hu, A. Xu, and C. Feng, "Semiconductor Metal Oxides as Chemoresistive Sensors for Detecting Volatile Organic Compounds," *Sensors*, vol. 19, no. 2, p. 233, Jan. 2019, doi: 10.3390/s19020233.

[9] D. A. Krawczyk, A. Rodero, K. Gładyszewska-Fiedoruk, and A. Gajewski, "CO 2 concentration in naturally ventilated classrooms located in different climates—Measurements and simulations," *Energy and Buildings*, vol. 129, pp. 491–498, Oct. 2016, doi: 10.1016/j.enbuild.2016.08.003.

[10] Bosch, "Low power gas, pressure, temperature & humidity sensor," BME680 datasheet, Rev. 1.6, Jan. 2021. Accessed Jun. 08, 2021. [Online]. Available: https://www.bosch-sensortec.com/media/boschsensortec/downloads/datasheets/bst-bme680-ds001.pdf.

[11] Bosch, "Integration Guide," Bosch software Environmental Cluster (BSEC), Jun. 2020. Accessed Jun. 08, 2021. [Online]. Available: https://www.bosch-sensortec.com/software-tools/software/bsec/.

[12] "Nanopb - protocol buffers with small code size." https://jpa.kapsi.fi/nanopb/ (accessed Jun. 08, 2021).

[13] *Energetische Bewertung von Gebäuden - Lüftung von Gebäuden - Teil 1: Eingangsparameter für das Innenraumklima zur Auslegung und Bewertung der Energieeffizienz von Gebäuden bezüglich Raumluftqualität, Temperatur, Licht und Akustik - Modul M1-6*, DIN EN 16798-1:2021-04, Deutsches Institut für Normung, Berlin, Germany, Apr. 2021.

[14] "Carbon dioxide levels continue at record levels, despite COVID-19 lockdown," World Meteorological Organization, Nov. 20, 2020. https://public.wmo.int/en/media/press-release/carbon-dioxide-levels-continue-record-levels-despite-covid-19-lockdown (accessed Jun. 08, 2021).

[15] "InfluxDB contains everything you need in a time series data platform in a single binary" https://www.influxdata.com/products/influxdb (accessed Jun. 08, 2021).

[16] "InfluxDB key concepts" https://docs.influxdata.com/influxdb/v2.0/reference/key-concepts (accessed Jun. 08, 2021).

[17] "Grafana Labs, "Grafana Features", [Online] Available: https://grafana.com/grafana/ (accessed Jun. 08, 2021).

[18] R. Menghi, S. Ceccacci, A. Papetti, M. Marconi, and M. Germani, "A method to estimate the total VOC emission of furniture products," *Procedia Manufacturing*, vol. 21, pp. 486–493, Jan. 2018, doi: 10.1016/j.promfg.2018.02.148.

[19] W. W. Nazaroff and C. J. Weschler, "Cleaning products and air fresheners: exposure to primary and secondary air pollutants," *Atmospheric Environment*, vol. 38, no. 18, pp. 2841–2865, Jun. 2004, doi: 10.1016/j.atmosenv.2004.02.040.

[20] T. Hussein and M. Kulmala, "Indoor Aerosol Modeling: Basic Principles and Practical Applications," *Water Air Soil Pollut: Focus*, vol. 8, pp. 23–34, 2008, https://doi.org/10.1007/s11267-007-9134-x.

[21] I. Salma *et al.*, "Physical properties, chemical composition, sources, spatial distribution and sinks of indoor aerosol particles in a university lecture hall," *Atmospheric Environment*, vol. 64, pp. 219–228, 2013, https://doi.org/10.1016/j.atmosenv.2012.09.070.

[22] A. M. Yeoman *et al.*, "Simplified speciation and atmospheric volatile organic compound emission rates from non-aerosol personal care products," *Indoor Air*, vol. 30, no. 3, pp. 459–472, 2020, doi: https://doi.org/10.1111/ina.12652.

[23] E. J. Kirkland, Advanced computing in electron microscopy, Second edition. New York: Springer, 2010.

[24] M. A. Oliver and R. Webster, "A tutorial guide to geostatistics: Computing and modelling variograms and kriging," *CATENA*, vol. 113, pp. 56–69, Feb. 2014, doi: 10.1016/j.catena.2013.09.006.

[25] H. Hagen and D. Roller, Geometric Modeling: Methods and Applications. Berlin, Heidelberg: Springer Berlin Heidelberg, 1991.

[26] Z. Li, K. Wang, H. Ma, and Y. Wu, "An Adjusted Inverse Distance Weighted Spatial Interpolation Method," in *Proc. 3rd Int. Con. Communications, Information Management and Network Security*, Nov. 2018, pp. 128-132, doi: 10.2991/cimns-18.2018.29.

[27] M. Buhmann and J. Jäger, "On radial basis functions," *Snapshots of modern mathematics*, p. 02, 2019, doi: 10.14760/SNAP-2019-002-EN.

# Ozone Sensors Based on $WO_3$ Sputtered Layers Enhanced by Ultra Violet Light Illumination

Clément Occelli, Sandrine Bernardini, Ludovic Le Roy, Tomas Fiorido, Jean-Luc Seguin and Carine Perrin-Pellegrino
Aix Marseille Univ, Université de Toulon, CNRS, IM2NP, AMUtech Institute, Marseille, France
e-mails : {clement.occelli, sandrine.bernardini, ludovic.leroy, tomas.fiorido, j-l.seguin and carine.perrin-pellegrino} @im2np.fr

***Abstract*—In this work, the conductance behavior of tungsten trioxide based chemoresistive ozone sensors under ultra violet illumination was investigated. The tungsten trioxide sensitive layers were deposited on a $SiO_2$/Si substrate by reactive radio frequency magnetron sputtering with several Argon / Oxygen ratios. The detection principle is based on a change in the conductance of the semiconductor oxides when ozone is present around the surface. We demonstrate the influence of Argon / Oxygen during the deposition of the sensitive layer, on ozone detection at 50°C under light illumination. The sensor shows good sensitivity to ozone, with a stable baseline, fast response and recovery time. These results are promising for the detection of ozone at low temperature.**

***Keywords-Gas sensors; UV activation; Electronic traps; Ozone; Environment; Health.***

## I. INTRODUCTION

Tungsten trioxide ($WO_3$) sensitive layers have been shown to be an effective material for ozone ($O_3$) detection [1]. Metal oxides present good sensitivity, long term stability and low cost production. However, their high operating temperature (around 280°C) is a drawback, as it increases their power consumption, affects the ageing of the materials and compromises their use on flexible substrates. Nevertheless, some metal oxides, such as zinc oxide (ZnO) or $WO_3$, exhibit photo-catalytic behavior [2]-[3] which can lower their optimal detection temperature by supplying them with energy in the form of Ultra Violet (UV) light radiation. This work is dedicated to experimental detection of ozone at 50°C under UV illumination using a $WO_3$ sensing layer. The paper is structured as follows: in Section II, we will describe the sensors and the experimental set up; then, in Section III, the sensing results will be discussed based on our measurements in dark and under UV light illumination in ozone environments. Finally, a conclusion is drawn in Section IV.

## II. DESCRIPTION OF APPROACH AND TECHNIQUES

This section is composed of two parts: one section is dedicated to the sensing film fabrication, while the other is devoted to the measurement system set-up.

### A. Gas sensors

The gas sensor is based on a transducer made of Ti/Pt interdigitated electrodes (5 and 100 nm thick, respectively) spaced by 50 μm (Figure 1) deposited on $Si/SiO_2$ substrate. The $WO_3$ sensitive layer, about 50 nm thick, was deposited by reactive Radio Frequency (RF) magnetron sputtering. The Argon (Ar) / Oxygen ($O_2$) ratio was changed as shown in Table I. All samples were deposited at a power of 115 W under a total pressure of $3.10^{-3}$ mbar.

TABLE I. ARGON / OXYGEN PLASMA RATIO OF SAMPLES PREPARED BY RF SPUTTERING

| Samples | *EC* | *EB* | *ED* |
|---|---|---|---|
| $Ar/O_2$ ratio | 3 : 2 | 1 : 1 | 2 : 3 |

All these samples, named EC, EB and ED series in our experiments, were then annealed in ambient air at a temperature of 400°C for two hours to improve their nano-crystallization and stability.

Figure 1. Sample image of $SiO_2$/Si substrate (4 x 4 mm$^2$) with platinum electrodes and a trioxide tungsten layer above it

The film structures were determined by X-Ray Diffraction (XRD) with a Philip's X'Pert MPD equipment (λ = 1.54 Å). Chemical composition measurement was performed using Energy Dispersive X-ray Spectroscopy (EDS) on a Zeiss GeminiSEM 500 ultra high resolution Field Emission Scanning Electron Microscope (FESEM). An Energy dispersive analysis of X-rays (EDAX) Octane Silicon Drift Detector (129 eV energy resolution for Manganese) was used at 5 kV with a magnificence of 350 and 10k.

### B. Experimental Setup for Sensor Characterization

Our test bench consists of a gas generation unit, a test chamber with a Light Emitting Diode (LED UV5TZ-390-30) and a Keithley Model 2450 Source Measure Unit (SMU) (Keithley, U.S.A.) monitored by a homemade LabVIEW program. The gas sensing properties were investigated by measuring the microsensor resistance in a closed thermo-regulated test chamber. The experimental set-up allows the sensors to be tested in dry air and diluted gas. Ozone is produced with an $O_3$ generator model 165 from Thermo Environmental Instruments and its concentration is measured using an $O_3$ analyzer model 49 from Thermo Environmental Instruments. In all experiments, the gas flow rate was maintained at 500 sccm (Standard Cubic Centimeters per Minute). For each concentration, the sensors were exposed to the gas for 60 s and their temperature was kept constant at 50°C. The distance between the UV LED and the microsensor was kept constant to allow a 1.5 mW/cm$^2$ measured power density at the sensor surface. Figure 2 shows a sensor under irradiation from a UV LED.

Figure 2. A sensor under UV illumination.

## III. Results and Discussions

The experiments were conducted in a laboratory environment. In this section, we will discuss our morphological and electrical results.

### A. Chemical Composition

The XRD diffractograms of $WO_3$ films (Figure 3) show the presence of crystalline layers with monoclinic phase $WO_3$ [4].

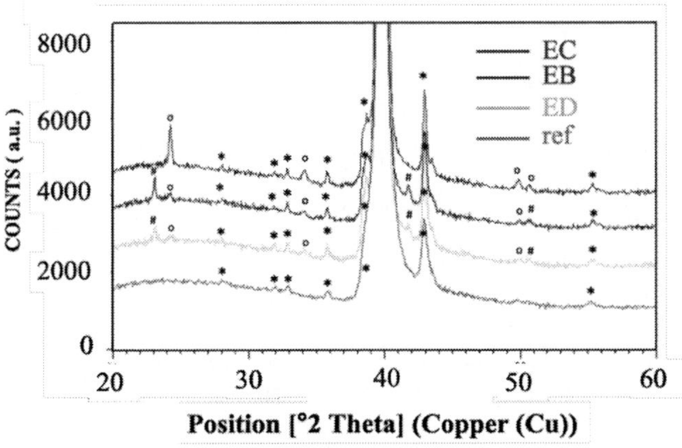


Figure 3. Comparison of $WO_3$ diffractograms with reference test platform (*) using λ = 1.54Å (Philip's X'Pert MRD).

A diffractogram was performed on the test platform with the interdigitated electrodes (Ti/Pt) deposited on $SiO_2$/Si substrate without the trioxide layer, to be used as a reference diffractogram. The diffractogram comparison of the samples with the metal oxide layers demonstrates the presence of two grain orientation families, identified on the figure 3 with the symbols # and o. All the diffraction peaks are compatible with the monoclinic structure of $WO_3$. But it seems that depending on the Ar/$O_2$ ratio used during the sputtering, the growth of grains with different orientations are favored. Particularly, the lowest oxygen ratio sample (EC) does not present the peaks identified on the figure as #. Three EDX measurements were carried out on the same sample at two different magnifications: x350 on $WO_3$ on three different electrodes and x10,000 on $WO_3$ on one electrode. The analyzed areas were 3 µm by 3 µm. To avoid the $SiO_2$ interferences on our $WO_3$ chemical measurements, preliminary tests were performed on platinum electrodes. A 5 kV electron beam energy was used for all the analysis. Energy Dispersive X-Ray (EDX) Spectroscopy measurements show that for this electron beam energy and 100 nm thick platinum electrode, no silicon element was detected. Thus, by performing our measurements on $WO_3$ with a platinum electrode underneath, no incertitude was induced by the $SiO_2$ substrate. When analyzing these results, no clear variation was observed on the chemical composition of the films for both magnifications. The $WO_3$ material maintains a near-stoichiometric composition over the whole deposition range with a ratio of nearly 77%O and 23%W (standard deviation of 0.5%). Auger electron spectroscopy (AES) analyses carried out in another study [5] demonstrated that the O/W ratio can indeed be altered by varying the oxygen content of the plasma, but that after annealing in air, the disparities tend to disappear. Thus, whatever the oxygen value used in our plasma, a quasi-stoichiometric ratio was observed. These results are in agreement with literature [5]-[8] where X-Ray Photoelectron Spectroscopy (XPS) analyses of $WO_3$ layers deposited under several conditions show that the chemical composition of $WO_3$ remains stoichiometric unless other chemical species are used during the annealing.

### B. Gas Detection under UV illumination

Semiconducting metal oxides are the most commonly used sensing materials for gas detection. They are cheap, stable, highly sensitive and need low maintenance. Nevertheless, energy activation is required to facilitate the chemical reaction on their surface and induce a change in carrier concentration upon exposure to gas molecules. Thus, their electrical conductance changes. In this work, we used a light activation to study the $WO_3$ photocatalytic properties at 50°C. The effect of visible and UV lights on the detection properties of $WO_3$ can be described as the result of two mechanisms. The first one occurs at low photon energies. Oxygen ions ($O_2^-$) are chemically bound to the surface with the free charge carriers of the material, electrons. This binding is of the order of 1.50 eV. Therefore, when the $WO_3$ surface is irradiated by a photon source with an energy higher than 1.50 eV, oxygen species capture the photons and desorption occurs, releasing charge carriers and increasing the conductance of the material. This increase is generally small (drop is less than a factor of 10 in the resistance) and does not allow for rapid and repeatable detection. The second mechanism is added when the photon energies are higher than the indirect band gap of $WO_3$, of the order of 2.6-2.8 eV: the creation of electron-hole pairs. These pairs increase the density of free charge carriers and participate in the desorption of oxygen atoms [9]-[11]. A large increase in conductivity is achieved (about a factor of $10^2 - 10^3$) and a large proportion of surface sites are unoccupied. Upon injection of ozone into the test chamber, the reactive gas molecules begin to occupy the free surface sites and bind to the free charge carriers, creating a depletion zone that increases the resistivity. Figure 4 shows a UV LED spectrum produced by our Avantes spectrometry equipment at room temperature (25°C).

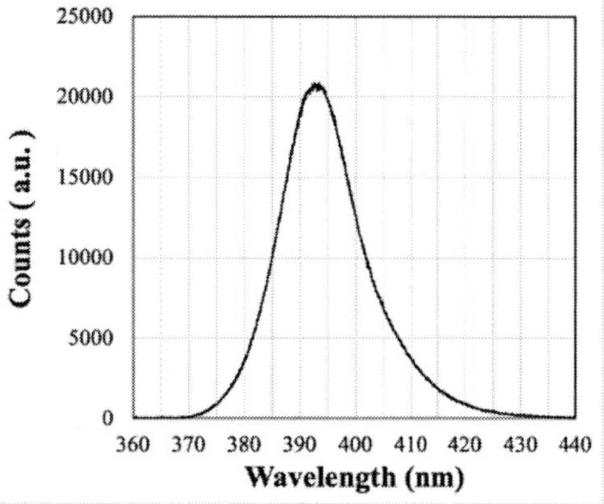


Figure 4. UV LED Spectrum

We observe a broad peak centered at 393 nm corresponding to the UV LED used in our experiments. The maximum intensity is reached around 393 nm which corresponds to a maximum energy of 3.16 eV calculated with formula (1):

$$E = h^*c / \lambda \tag{1}$$

where h is the Planck constant, c the light speed and λ the wavelength.

Thus, according to the literature, there is both desorption of oxygen and creation of electron-hole pair. This hypothesis was confirmed by the decrease in resistance when our sensor was exposed to UV light.

The normalized response of the sensor is defined in (2) as the ratio of the sensor resistance under the $O_3$ exposure to the sensor resistance in dry air:

$$R = R_{gas} / R_{air} \tag{2}$$

where $R_{air}$ is the sensor resistance through dry airflow and $R_{gas}$ the sensor resistance in the presence of $O_3$.

Figure 5 shows the detection properties towards $O_3$ of the EB sample made with an $Ar/O_2$ gas ratio 1:1, as generally reported in the literature [7], [12] under UV light and darkness.

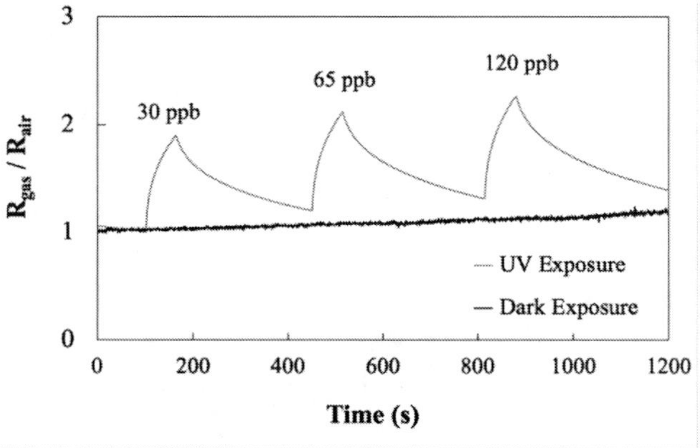


Figure 5. Ozone detection, at an operating temperature of 50°C, in dark and under UV illumination for a $WO_3$ film prepared with a 1:1 $Ar/O_2$ ratio.

In darkness and at low temperature maintained at 50°C, the optimal conditions for chemisorption reaction are not reached, so no adsorption or desorption of oxygen species ($O^{2-}$ or $O_3$) can occur. The "Dark Exposure" curve shows a constant baseline and no response is observed for all ozone exposures of 30 ppb, 65 ppb and 120 ppb, respectively. Under UV illumination and at 50°C, desorption of $O^{2-}$ by absorption of UV photon occurs and electron-hole pairs are created, thus chemical reaction becomes possible. The "UV Exposure" plot indicates a normalized response of 1.89, 2.10 and 2.25 reached for 60 s ozone exposure at 30 ppb, 65 ppb and 120 ppb, respectively. Stabilization was incomplete for response and recovery as chemisorption remains a slow process and ten minutes were generally required [9], [13].

Figure 6 illustrates the sensors responses to 30 ppb ozone for several $Ar/O_2$ gas ratios in the sputtering deposition process.

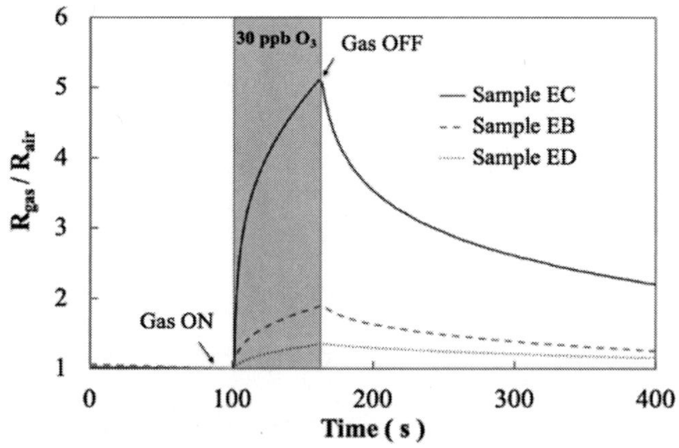


Figure 6. Comparison of Ozone (30 ppb) detection by our samples. Measurements under UV illumination for an operating temperature equals to 50°C.

The EB sample made with an Ar /$O_2$ gas ratio of 1:1 shows a response of 1.89 for an ozone concentration of 30 ppb. By increasing the oxygen content during the plasma process, the sensor response to ozone is found to decrease, and a normalized response of 1.35 is achieved for 30 ppb of $O_3$. On the contrary, by decreasing the oxygen content, the sensor response to ozone increases, and a normalized response of 5.10 is achieved for 30 ppb of $O_3$.This trend is maintained for other ozone concentrations as show in figure 7.

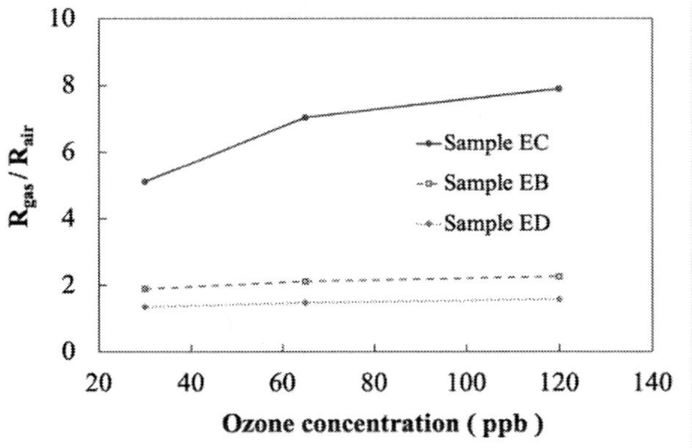


Figure 7. Response of three sensors to ozone concentration variation, under UV illumination at an operating temperature of 50°C.

The lowest oxygen ratio sample has the highest normalized response to ozone of 5.10, 7.04 and 7.90, which is promising for ozone detection at low temperature, while the highest argon ratio sample has the lowest normalized response of 1.35, 1.47 and 1.59 for 30 ppb, 65 ppb and 120 ppb, respectively.

## IV. Conclusion And Future Work

This work reports our preliminary results on ozone sensors, based on a $WO_3$ sputtering layer, operating at 50°C under UV light detection. Our results demonstrated that the Ar/$O_2$ ratio used during the layer deposition did not affecting the chemical stoichiometry after annealing at 400°C during 2 h. However, XRD measurements showed that several preferential grain orientations were formed during the layer fabrication depending on the Ar/$O_2$ ratio during the $WO_3$ sensitive layer deposition. Our results demonstrate that the choice of the best Ar/$O_2$ ratio during the $WO_3$ sensitive layer fabrication will allow to optimize the ozone detection at low temperature by light illumination. Complementary XPS measurements will be performed to understand the influence of oxygen vacancy on our results.

## Acknowledgment

The work was supported by the AMUtech Institute via a master student grant. We would like to thank Andrea Campos for her technical support and comments.

## References

[1] J. Guérin, K. Aguir, and M. Bendahan, 'Modeling of the conduction in a $WO_3$ thin film as ozone sensor', Sensors and Actuators B: Chemical, Volume 119, Issue 1, 24, pp. 327-334, 2006, doi.org/10.1016/j.snb.2005.12.005

[2] E. Comini, G. Faglia, and G. Sberveglieri, 'UV light activation of tin oxide thin films for $NO_2$ sensing at low temperatures', Sensors and Actuators B: Chemical 78 pp. 73–77, 2001, doi.org/10.1016/S0925-4005(01)00796-1

[3] L.F da Silva, *et al.*, 'UV-enhanced ozone gas sensing response of ZnO-$SnO_2$ heterojunctions at room temperature, Sensors and Actuators B: Chemical, 240, pp. 573-579, 2017 doi.org/10.1016/j.snb.2016.08.158

[4] The International Center for Diffraction Data, Newton Square, $WO_3$ card number 00-43-1035, $WO_3$ Card Number 00-43-1035. 2002

[5] C. Lemire, D. B. B. Lollman, A. Al Mohammad, E. Gillet, and K. Aguir, 'Reactive R.F. magnetron sputtering deposition of $WO_3$ thin films', Sensors and Actuators B: Chemical, vol. 84, no. 1, pp. 43–48, 2002, doi: 10.1016/S0925-4005(02)00009-6

[6] I. M. Szilágyi, *et al.*, '$WO_3$ photocatalysts: Influence of structure and composition', Journal of Catalysis, vol. 294, pp. 119–127, 2012, doi: 10.1016/j.jcat.2012.07.013

[7] I. Castro-Hurtado, T. Tavera, P. Yurrita, N. Pérez, A. Rodriguez, G.G. Mandayo, *et al.*, 'Structural and optical properties of $WO_3$ sputtered thin films nanostructured by laser interference lithography', Applied Surface Science, vol. 276, pp. 229–235, 2013, doi: 10.1016/j.apsusc.2013.03.072

[8] D.-S. Lee, K.-H. Nam, and D.-D. Lee, 'Effect of substrate on $NO_2$-sensing properties of $WO_3$ thin film gas sensors', Thin Solid Films, vol. 375, no. 1, pp. 142–146, 2000, doi: 10.1016/S0040-6090(00)01261-X

[9] C. Zhang, A. Boudiba, P. D. Marco, R. Snyders, M.-G. Olivier, and M. Debliquy, 'Room temperature responses of visible-light illuminated $WO_3$ sensors to $NO_2$ in sub-ppm range', Sensors and Actuators B: Chemical, vol. 181, pp. 395-401, 2013, doi: 10.1016/j.snb.2013.01.082

[10] E. Espid and F. Taghipour, 'UV-LED Photo-activated Chemical Gas Sensors: A Review', Critical Reviews in Solid State and Materials Sciences, vol. 42, no. 5, pp. 416–432, 2017, doi: 10.1080/10408436.2016.1226161

[11] A. Giberti, C. Malagù, and V. Guidi, '$WO_3$ sensing properties enhanced by UV illumination: An evidence of surface effect', Sensors and Actuators B: Chemical, vol. 165, no. 1, pp. 59–61, 2012, doi: 10.1016/j.snb.2012.02.012

[12] K. Khojier, H. Savaloni, N. Habashi, and M. H. Sadi, 'On the influence of temperature gradient of annealing process on the nanostructure and sensing properties of $WO_3$ thin films to $NO_2$ gas and relative humidity', Materials Science in Semiconductor Processing, vol. 41, pp. 177–183, 2016, doi: 10.1016/j.mssp.2015.08.036

[13] L. Giancaterini, *et al.*, 'The influence of thermal and visible light activation modes on the $NO_2$ response of $WO_3$ nanofibers prepared by electrospinning', Sensors and Actuators B: Chemical, vol. 229, pp. 387–395, 2016, doi: 10.1016/j.snb.2016.02.007

# SAW based $CO_2$ sensor: influence of functionalizing MOF crystal size on the sensor's selectivity.

Meddy Vanotti, Sacha Poisson, Virginie Blondeau-Patissier.
Time and Frequency Department (UMR CNRS 6174),
FEMTO-ST Institute,
26 Chemin de l'Epitaphe, 25030 Besançon Cedex, France.
e-mail : meddy.vanotti@femto-st.fr

Laurie André, Stéphane Brandès, Nicolas Desbois, Claude P. Gros.
Institut de Chimie Moléculaire de l'Université de Bourgogne (ICMUB, UMR CNRS 6302),
Université de Bourgogne Franche-Comté,
9 Avenue Alain Savary, BP 47870, 21078 Dijon Cedex, France.

***Abstract*— The potential impact of indoor air quality on human health has become an increasingly important topic of public health and, thus, has stimulated an interest in hazardous compounds survey such as carbon dioxide. To address this issue, we started the development of a Surface Acoustic Wave device functionalized with metal-organic framework for the selective detection of carbon dioxide. Here, we propose preliminary results on the influence of the size of the metal-organic framework crystals on the sensor's selectivity and on its evolution with the ageing of the sensor.**

***Keywords-Carbon dioxide sensor; SAW device; metal-organique framework.***

## I. Introduction

Road traffic considerably contributes to the exposure of human to air pollutants like carbon dioxide ($CO_2$). In traffic environments, the concentrations of traffic related pollutants are higher than in other environments and a considerable amount of time, on average from 4 % to 8 % of total hours of the day, is spent in traffic in developed countries. This points to the need for an air quality monitoring system in vehicle cabins, especially for $CO_2$. Here we propose preliminary results on a Surface acoustic Wave (SAW) based sensor for the selective detection of $CO_2$. In this work, we focus on the influence of the size of the ZnTACN Metal-Organic Framework (MOF) crystals used for the functionalization of its surface on the selectivity toward interferent such as carbon monoxide (CO) et oxygen ($O_2$). The evolution of the calculated selectivity with the ageing of the sensor is also discussed.

## II. Materials and Methods

We have developed a $CO_2$ sensor based on the potential of Surface Acoustic Waves (SAW) to probe mass variations [1] in $CO_2$ sensitive porous material. We used Love wave based SAW delay line built on a temperature compensated substrate of (YXlt)/36°/90° quartz. IDTs were made of aluminum and shaped by mean of a lift-off technique using negative photoresist. In order to allow the Love-mode acoustic wave to propagate at the surface of the device, a silica guiding layer was deposited on the top of the chip. We have selected a delay line configuration shown in Fig. 1 for the sensors because of the large functionalization area that it offers. Also, the robustness of such a device allows for the deposition of a sensitive layer compatible with its normal operating conditions [2, 3].

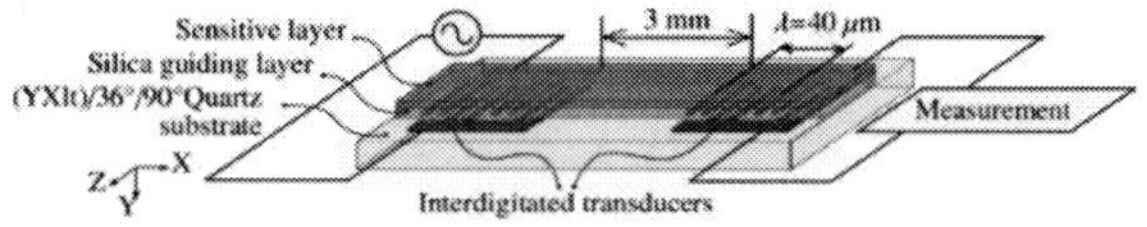


Figure 1. SAW device used for the manufacturing of the CO2 sensors.

The SAW device was than functionalized with metal-organic framework to reach sensitivity toward $CO_2$. The ZnTACN MOF represented in Fig. 2 was selected because of its high affinity with this gas described in the literature [4].

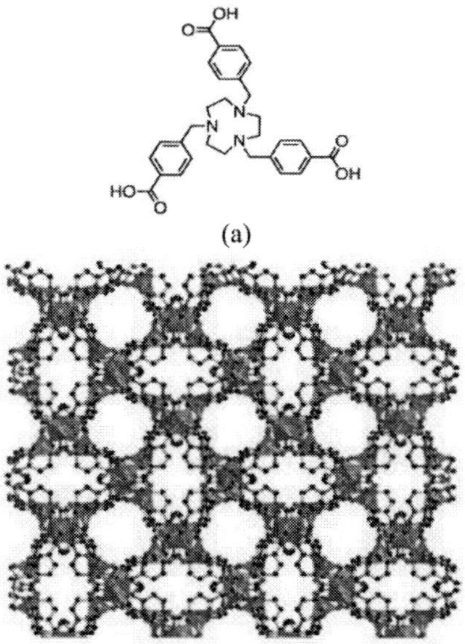


Figure 2. ZnTACN metal-organic framework (b) obtained by self assembly of TACN ligand (a) and zinc.

Depending on the scale of the synthesis, the crystals had sizes between 1 μm and 40 μm. The characteristic trigonal prismatic-like morphology with curved edges of the

ZnTACN MOF was observed by SEM assessing the proper synthesis and the functionalization of the surface (Fig. 3).

(a)

(b)

Figure 3. SEM images of the ZnTACN MOF with crystal size between 1.3 μm (a) and 40 μm (b).

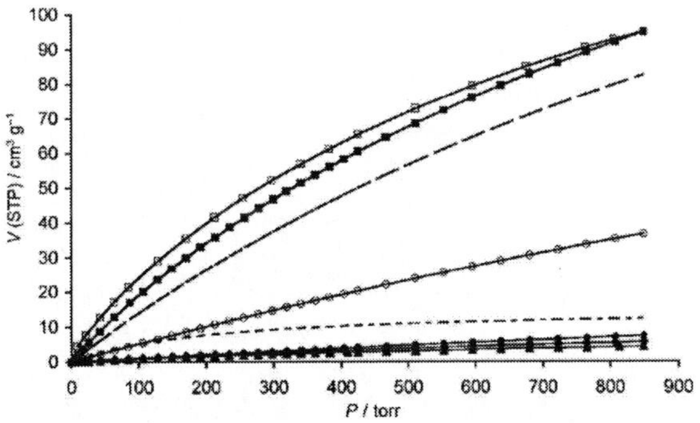


Figure 4. SEM Adsorption–desorption isotherms for ZnTACN MOF at 298 K with $CO_2$ (ads: ■, des: □), $CH_2$ (○), CO (●), $N_2$ (◆), and $O_2$ (▲).

The $CO_2$, CO, $CH_4$, $O_2$ and $N_2$ adsorption isotherms at 298 K are illustrated in Fig. 4. The thin solid lines are related to the calculated dual-site Langmuir isotherm model for $CO_2$ and single-site Langmuir-type isotherms for the other gases. Dashed and dotted lines indicate the two contributions for the calculated CO2 isotherm. The large uptake of CO2 compared to other gases, especially in the low-pressure range, clearly evidence the selective adsorption of $CO_2$. These isotherms were obtained with MOFs whose size is between 10 μm and 30 μm. Five sensors were coated with MOF of different sizes in the range [1-40] μm. SEM observations of the sensor's surface, shown on Fig. 3, were made to assess the presence of the MOF at the surface of the device and measure the crystal size. The evaluation of the coverage rate of the sensors was also made with a high-resolution digital microscope 4 K Serie VHX-7000 KEYENCE.

## III. RESULTS AND DISCUSSION

The sensors were exposed to $CO_2$, CO and $O_2$ diluted in pure $N_2$. The phase decrease observed during the exposures were characterized by means of the derived phase at the beginning of the phase decrease. This derived phase is referred to as 'Phase Shift Velocity' (PSV). This approach allows to measure gas concentration within a few tens of seconds [1]. The responses are normalized by the coverage rate of the sensor's surface and the gas concentration. The measurements of the three gases are plotted against the MOF crystals size in Fig. 5. It shows that the sensitivity of the sensor to $CO_2$ is inversely proportional to the crystal size. As expected from the adsorption isotherms presented in Fig. 4, the sensitivity to $O_2$ is virtually null. However, we observed an unexpected non-zero sensitivity to CO which tends to be linear with the MOF crystal size.

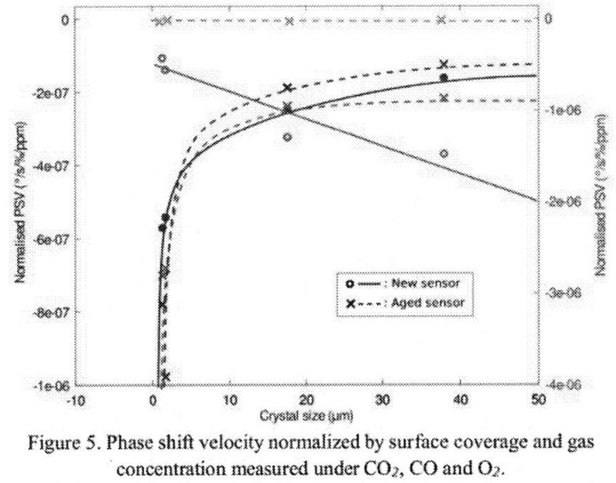


Figure 5. Phase shift velocity normalized by surface coverage and gas concentration measured under $CO_2$, CO and $O_2$.

On the basis of these measurements, we estimated that the CO2 vs O2 selectivity is virtually infinite since there is no measurable signal under O2. The CO2 vs CO selectivity was also calculated and plotted against the MOF crystals size on Fig. 6. It appears that is the case of brand-new sensor, the CO2 vs CO selectivity is inversely proportional to the MOF crystal size offering a potentially infinite selectivity in the submicronic range. However, in the studied range, its value isn't quite as high as expected from the measurement made on compacted powder (Fig. 4). This will draw our attention and further work will be engaged to explain the difference in the MOF sensitivity toward CO between the case of a compacted powder and the case of fewer crystals deposited on a surface. In the case of an aged sensor exposed to ambient air for days, the $CO_2$ vs CO selectivity dramatically decreases for small crystals. This behavior may be attributed to the breakdown of the zinc sites on the MOF structure after the exposure to ambient air.

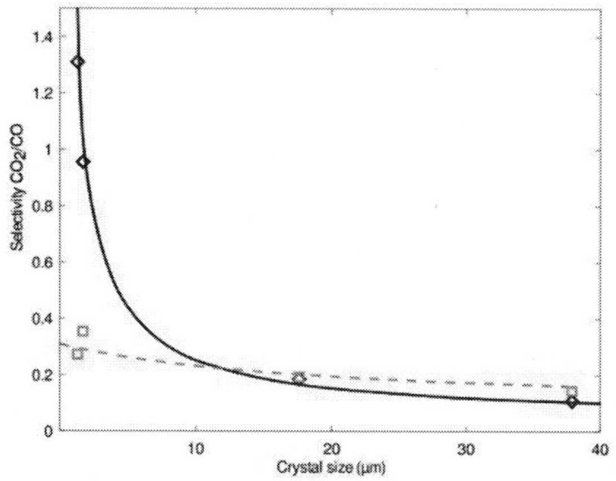


Figure 6. Selectivity CO2/CO versus MOF crystal size for new sensors and aged sensors.

## IV. CONCLUSIONS

In this work we showed the capability of a SAW based sensor functionalized with ZnTACN metal-organic framework to detect carbon dioxide. Although the measurements that were performed on compacted MOF powder showed high selectivity for $CO_2$ toward CO, we found a significantly lower selectivity for dispersed MOF crystals on the sensor's surface. More interestingly, we noticed a virtually infinite selectivity toward $O_2$ in the whole crystal size range and for submicronic crystals in the case of $CO_2$. These observations induce us to investigate further the potential of the ZnTACN MOF for the development of selective $CO_2$ sensor.

## ACKNOWLEDGMENT

This work was supported by the ISITE CO2DECIN (ANR-15-IDEX-0003), the European Union through the PO FEDER-FSE Bourgogne 2014/2020 (Convention n°2016-6200FE003S00257) via the CoMICS program, the French RENATECH network and its FEMTO-ST technological facility.

## REFERENCES

[1] M. Vanotti, S. Poisson, V. Soumann, V. Quesneau, S. Brandès, N. Desbois, Y. Yang, L. André, C.P. Gros, and V. Blondeau-Patissier. (2021). Influence of interfering gases on a carbon monoxide differential sensor based on SAW devices functionalized with cobalt and copper corroles. Sensors and Actuators B: Chemical, 332, 129507.

[2] M. Vanotti, V. Blondeau-Patissier, V. Moutarlier, and S. Ballandras, Analysis of palladium and yttrium–palladium alloy layers used for hydrogen detection with SAW device, Sens. Actuators B Chem. 217 (2015) 30–35, https://doi.org/10.1016/j.snb.2015.02.049.

[3] P. Zheng, T.-L. Chin, D. Greve, I. Oppenheim, V. Malone, T. Ashok, J. Miller, and L. Cao, Langasite SAW device with gas-sensitive layer, 2010 IEEE International Ultrasonics Symposium (2010) 1462–1465, https://doi.org/10.1109/ULTSYM.2010.5935779.

[4] G. Ortiz, S. Brandès, Y. Rousselin, and R. Guilard. (2011). Selective $CO_2$ Adsorption by a Triazacyclononane-Bridged Microporous Metalo-Organic Framework. Chemistry - A European Journal, 17(24), 6689-6695.G. Eason, B. Noble, and I. N. Sneddon, "On certain integrals of Lipschitz-Hankel type involving products of Bessel functions," Phil. Trans. Roy. Soc. London, vol. A247, pp. 529–551, April 1955.

# Development of a LoRa Wireless Sensor Network to Estimate Agricultural Risk

Maurício F. Lima Pereira,[1,2] Paulo E. Cruvinel[1,3]
[1]Embrapa Instrumentation, São Carlos, SP, Brazil
[2]Federal University of Mato Grosso – Computer Science Institute, Cuiabá, MT, Brazil
[3]Federal University of São Carlos – Post Graduation Program in Computer Science, São Carlos, SP, Brazil
Email: mauricio@ic.ufmt.br, paulo.cruvinel@embrapa.br

***Abstract*—Sensors are quite important for agricultural risk monitoring, and the customization of a LoRa wireless network and its use in rural applications is still a challenge. This paper presents a data collector system based on a Wi-Fi and Lora platform. The arrangement includes an ESP32, which is a single 2.4 GHz Wi-Fi and Bluetooth combo chip designed to operate with ultra-low-power and based on the 40 nm technologies. Therefore, the module allows using both protocols for Wi-Fi and LoRa wireless networks. One of the main characteristics, which was leveraged in this study, is its applicability for long-range communication in rural areas with low power consumption. During operation, the proposed receiver node is connected to the internet, thereby enabling data storage on servers, such as ThingSpeak, which is an Internet-of-Things analytics platform service. The results in a controlled-environment test showed that the connection between the station and receiver was fully functional at a distance of 500 meters. Besides, once this advanced data collector, currently under development, is finished, interconnection of several stations will be possible, even if they are remotely located with respect to the receiver node.**

***Index Terms*—*Agricultural Sensors; LPWAN; LoRa; Wireless Sensor Network***

## I. Introduction

Agribusiness is an important pillar of the Brazilian economy encompassing several areas. Automation has recently gained prominence in an area called precision and decision-making agriculture. In this scenario, the use of intelligent Global Positioning System (GPS) guided machines to plant, cultivate, and harvest accurately is growing in the most advanced areas of the country, achieving greater savings in inputs, productivity increase, and sustainability. Thus, it has become a driving force and an integrator within and outside the production chain.

In addition to the new technologies embedded in agricultural machinery, the development of low-cost agrometeorological stations and their connection by building a wireless network of sensors has proved to be useful in the field. This is because, based on the data generated by such equipment, computational techniques and statistics can be applied to extract useful information for the farmers.

In this context, the development of computational tools to support decisions based on these data is important to reduce risks and, consequently, losses in agricultural areas. Preliminary discussions about such subject have been presented in the regional meeting of Computer Brazilian Society [1]

Technologies to integrate microelectronics, collect and compute data, and evaluate field conditions based on agrometeorological data have been developed since the advent of microprocessors and advances in digital electronics [2]. More recently, however, the Internet-of-Things (IoT) has been playing a key role in Agriculture 4.0. Several types of sensors can be used for continuously measuring a great amount of data, assisted by wireless networks and cloud computing to create evaluation models for field conditions while providing greater safety for farmers [3].

An important application for sensors in agriculture is directly measuring soil characteristics through parameters such as pH, nutrient content, temperature, and moisture, among other variables of interest.

The results of soil evaluation are important for obtaining a more precise scenario of the planting area and, therefore, higher performance and quality. Advanced technology systems are thus necessary for high-performance yields [4].

Based on this scenario, Figure 1 shows an adaptation of the structure to agricultural risk models proposed by Cruvinel and collaborators [5]. In such context, the developed method exploits smart sensors to measure Soil Quality (SQ) indicators.

SQ is one of the factors that influence agricultural risk given that it can influence the productivity indexes of crops [6]–[9].

In such a context, different protocols for data communication have been observed in the literature. One example is the LoRaWAN protocol, which can enable implementation for long-range networks, avoiding the use of conventional cellular networks, whose coverage in Brazil in rural areas is still not ideal.

As part of a broader project in which the development of agricultural-risk analysis tools based on data from different sources is being developed, this study presents a new approach of both climatical and soil data collector system based on a wireless network, which is intended to be one of those data-sources for support decision making in agricultural risk [10]–[12].

The remainder of the paper is organized as follows: Section II presents the materials and methods; Section III presents the results and discussions; finally, conclusion and future studies are presented in Section IV.

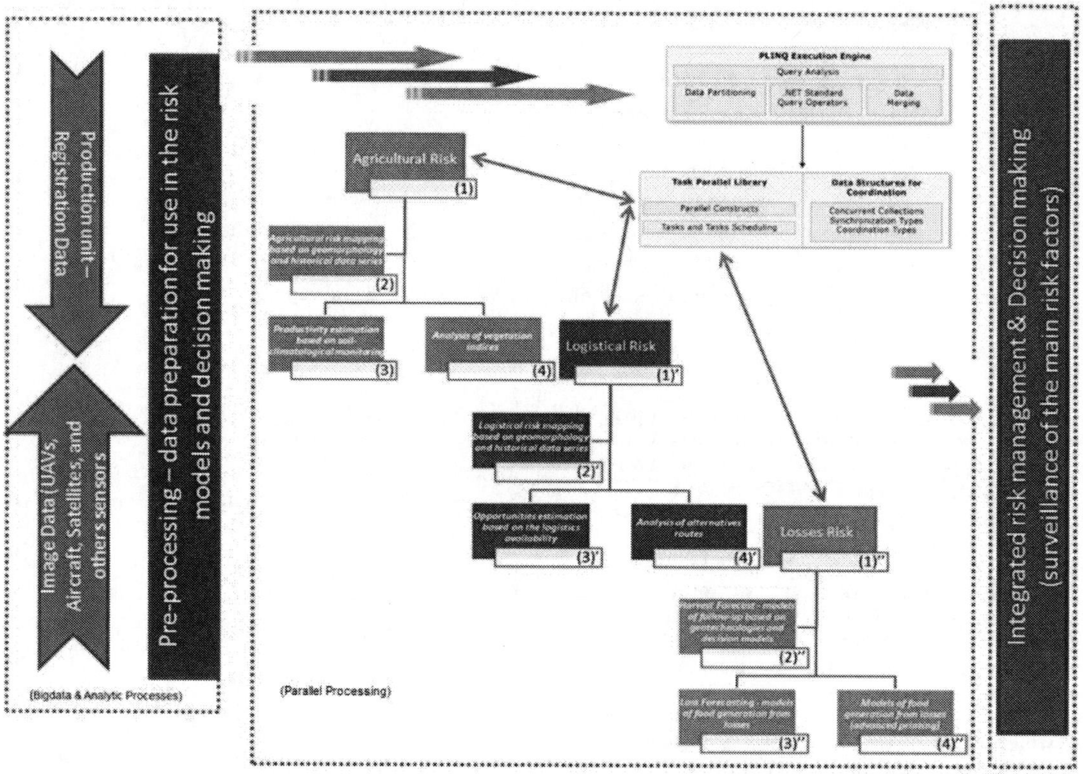


Figure 1. A framework related to the use of geo-technologies and embedded support decision systems for agricultural risk management.

## II. Materials and Methods

A hardware device based on Arduino Mega 2560 was used to build the first version of the data collector equipment, connecting sensors to a Heltec Wi-Fi Lora 32 [13], which contains an ESP32 micro-controller, a Bluetooth low-energy transmitter, a Wi-Fi transmitter, and a LoRa transmitter, in a single board. Both boards exchange information through their serial ports. Data were also received using a Heltec Wi-Fi LoRa 32 module. The equipment receives, organizes, and transmits data to a remote server using a dedicated Wi-Fi network. In the first sensor validation stage, data from stations were stored in ThingSpeak, an IoT platform that enables real-time aggregation, visualization, and analysis of data flows in the cloud. Air temperature, humidity, wind speed and rainfall were initially monitored. Data were also inserted into a Mosquitto, NodeRed, and Postgres-based platform, which will be integrated in a high-performance architecture using Apache-Spark to treat and process data through a risk calculation algorithm [14].

Figure 2 presents the basic architecture developed for soil quality risk analysis, in which it is possible to observe not only the model components but also the LoRa structure and protocol used for wireless agricultural data communication.

Figure 3 presents the developed concept: a station containing microprocessors, a DS DHT22 sensor, a bascule pluviometer [15], and an anemometer. Another Wi-Fi LoRa module was positioned 500 meters away playing the role of a gateway, receiving data from the station and transmitting them to ThingSpeak through a dedicated Wi-Fi network.

The following sections describe the experimental organization of the equipment, the hardware used for the collector system, a brief notion about LoRa networks, and the organization of the station firmware.

### A. *Area and agricultural experiment*

The collector system prototype was installed inside a reserved area of the National Precision Agriculture Reference Laboratory (Lanapre) from the Embrapa Agricultural Instrumentation Center, São Carlos, Brazil, aiming to build a database to validate risk calculation models. The agricultural area was about 80 by 50 meters, having corn (*Zea mays.*) planted throughout its extension. The area was divided into 4 plots measuring 20 meters by 50 meters each. Their soil will receive different amounts of nitrogen; the soil and plants will be measured over time. As presented in Figure 4(a), the first plot did not receive nitrogen at all (0%), the second received 50% of the amount recommended in the literature, the third received 100% of the recommended amount, and the fourth received 200% of that amount. Soil samples were extracted in three growth stages along the crop cycle from three depths: 0-20, 20-40, and 40-60 centimeters.

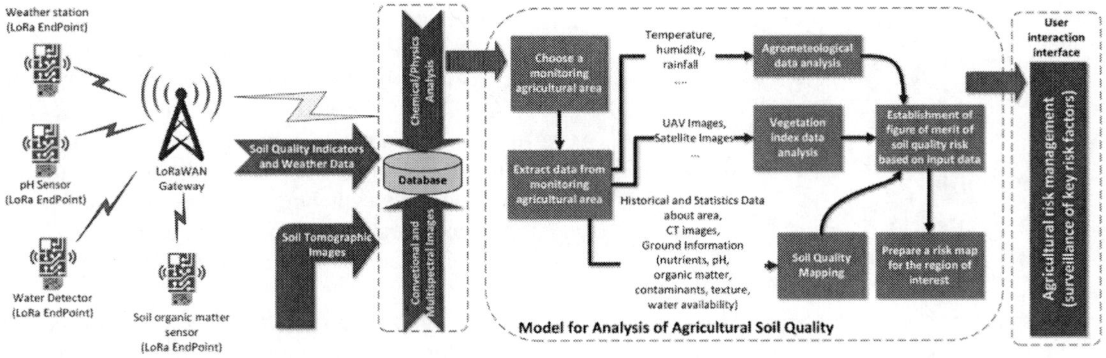


Figure 2. Soil quality risk management based on wireless communication and embedded systems for decision support.

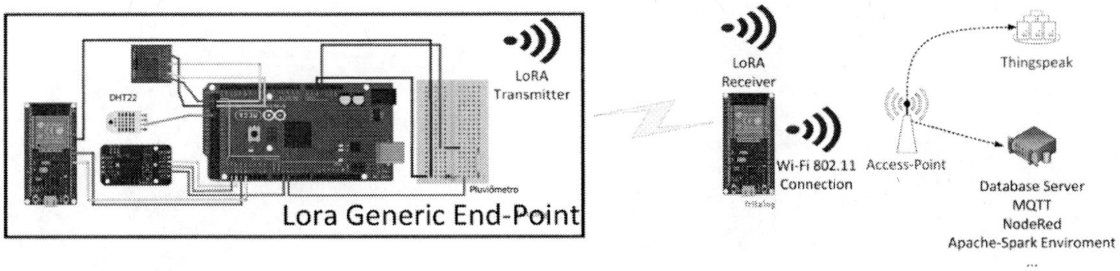


Figure 3. Prototype of data collector device based on Arduino Mega and Heltec automation using LoRa to transmit agrometeorological data in the field.

The collector system has obtained climate data over a prescribed experimental period from temperature, humidity, wind speed, and rainfall sensors to build more accurate agricultural risk models. The objective was to integrate those pieces of information into an agricultural-risk analysis model. Figure 4(b) shows the experimental area with corn planted according to the experiment plan. In addition to various climate variables from the planting stage, aerial images were extracted from drones equipped with multi-spectral cameras. The resulting images also composed the dataset used in the high-performance processing platform.

### *B. LoRa and LoRaWAN*

LoRa (long-range) is a patented modulation technology for wireless communications acquired by Semtech Corporation in 2012 [16] [17].

LoRa is a wireless solution for networks below 1 GHz. It uses frequencies that demand no licensing, e.g., 433, 868, and 915 MHz. This type of networks is used to connect devices in low-consumption long-range applications because it can reach 15 km in open field [18].

A remarkable advantage of LoRa is the high sensitivity of its sensor and the great capacity of its communication link, allowing long-range transmissions. Typical SNR levels for spreading factors 10 and 12 when using LoRa modulation are -20 dB and -15 dB, obtaining receiver sensitivities of -134 dBm and -129 dBm, respectively. These values are barely comparable to the typical sensitivity of Wi-Fi or Bluetooth receivers, which is often in the range from -40 dBm to -80 dBm. The main properties of LoRa modulation are 1) its scalable bandwidth and frequency, enabling easy change from narrowband to wideband hopping, 2) resistance to Doppler shift, 3) relatively high immunity to fading or multi-path, especially in dense scenarios, and 4) robustness to interference.

The LoRa specification just provides the physical layer for radio communication. Besides, the LoRaWAN is the most popular protocol for wide area networks and it is, fundamentally, a network protocol designed with a special focus on battery-powered devices, as they are the most commonly used devices with LoRA. Therefore, energy consumption must be kept as low as possible. The network topology of LoRaWAN is a star network, in which several end-devices transmit to a given gateway. In fact, devices broadcast their transmissions, which might be received by several gateways. Then, backend servers, which all gateways are connected to, make an automatic decision on which gateway manages the received packets. Uplink transmissions are considered predominant in LoRaWAN, and therefore have preference over downlink connections. The protocol addresses this aspect by defining three different classes of connected end-devices with an incremental number of features: (1) Class-A devices, with the basic set of features that all devices must implement; (2) Class-B devices, with scheduled listening windows; and (3) Class-C devices, for bi-directional communication at any time [19]–[22]. To meet the different requirements of a wide range of IoT applications, the LoRaWAN communication protocol offers three class types for sending and receiving packets, as shown in Figure 5.

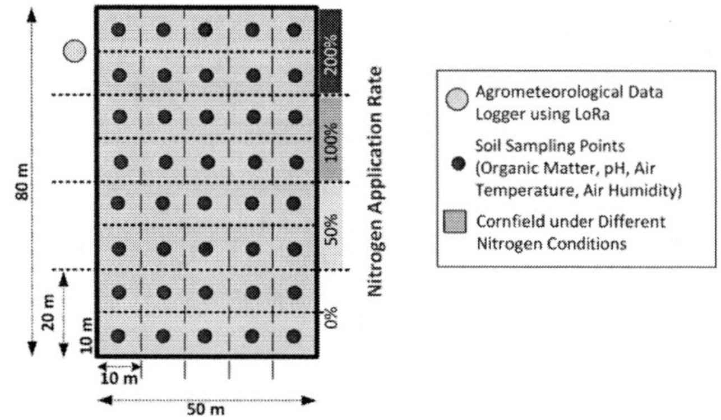


(a)

(b)

Figure 4. Experimental area: (a) Design of the plots using an agricultural data collector system; (b) Corn crop (*Zea mays.*) according to the plan.

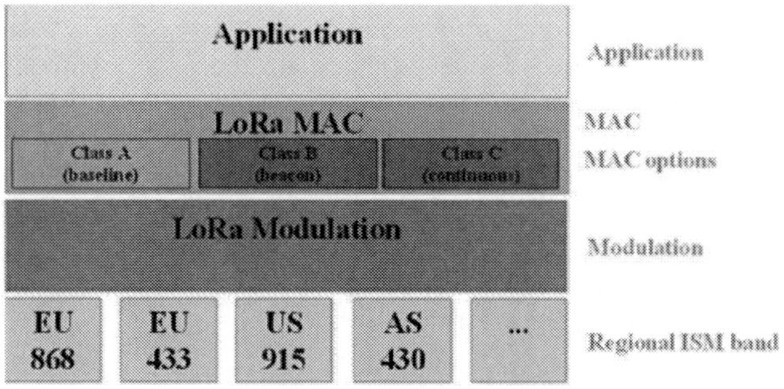


Figure 5. LoRaWAN Classes [23].

## C. Heltec Wi-Fi Lora 32 Module

The Heltec Wi-Fi LoRa 32 module presented in Figure 6 stands out for its ESP32 processor from Espressif [24] with a 32-bit Reduced Instruction Set Computer (RISC) architecture, and its dual-processing ultra-low-power core. The SX1276/SX1278 LoRa chip [25] is also attached to the module, enabling connections using this type of network. In addition to LoRa, the module includes Wi-Fi and Bluetooth connections through their respective antennas. An IPEX interface is available to connect an external antenna for LoRa.

An SH1.25-2 battery interface in the lower portion of the module with an integrated lithium battery management system allows controlling charging and discharging, protecting against overload, and switching between USB and battery sources. The module also has a 0.96 inch, 128 x 64, organic light-emitting diode (OLED) display on the top for programming and operating.

The manufacturer provides libraries for programming in the native Arduino environment, Platformio, and Visual Code.

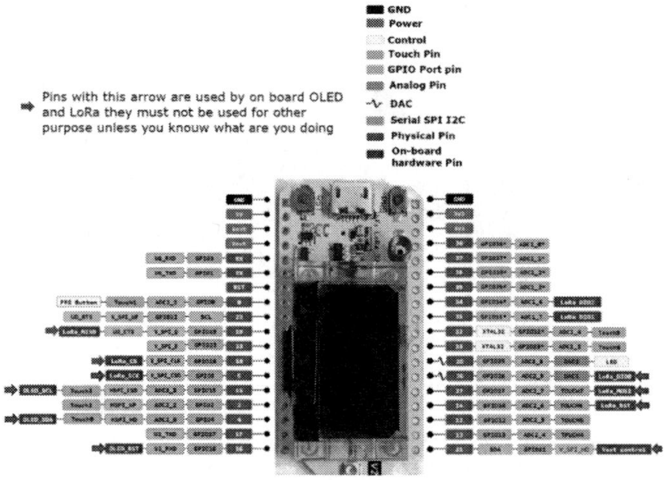


Figure 6. Heltec Wi-Fi 32 LoRa module pinout.

## D. Structure of the collector station firmware

All sensors, the Real Time Clock DS3231, and non-volatile memory modules were connected to Arduino Mega 2560, while the Heltec Wi-Fi LoRa 32 module managed communication tasks. Therefore, all the data collection was programmed into Arduino's firmware. At first, the firmware used the interrupt ports to facilitate processing. The pluviometer interrupts when a new pulse is detected, which occurs when its inner recipient reaches a 0.25-mm rain volume, and moves the weighbridge, generating a 5-V signal in port 47 of the Arduino, which interrupts its activity to record a flag and an increment in the number of pulses. The DS3231 was programmed to fire once a minute in the same firmware, and all the events of information data collection from the DHT22, anemometer, and rainfall were coordinated by this signal, which also determined when the information had to be packed and sent through the serial port to the LoRa-WiFi module. The same data were recorded into the memory card to increase safety.

The Heltec module received data through the serial port and communicated with the receiving module, sending the packages from Arduino. The Wi-Fi and Bluetooth networks remained switched off in this module for consumption purposes. Figure 7 presents the algorithm structure and the parallel execution of each module.

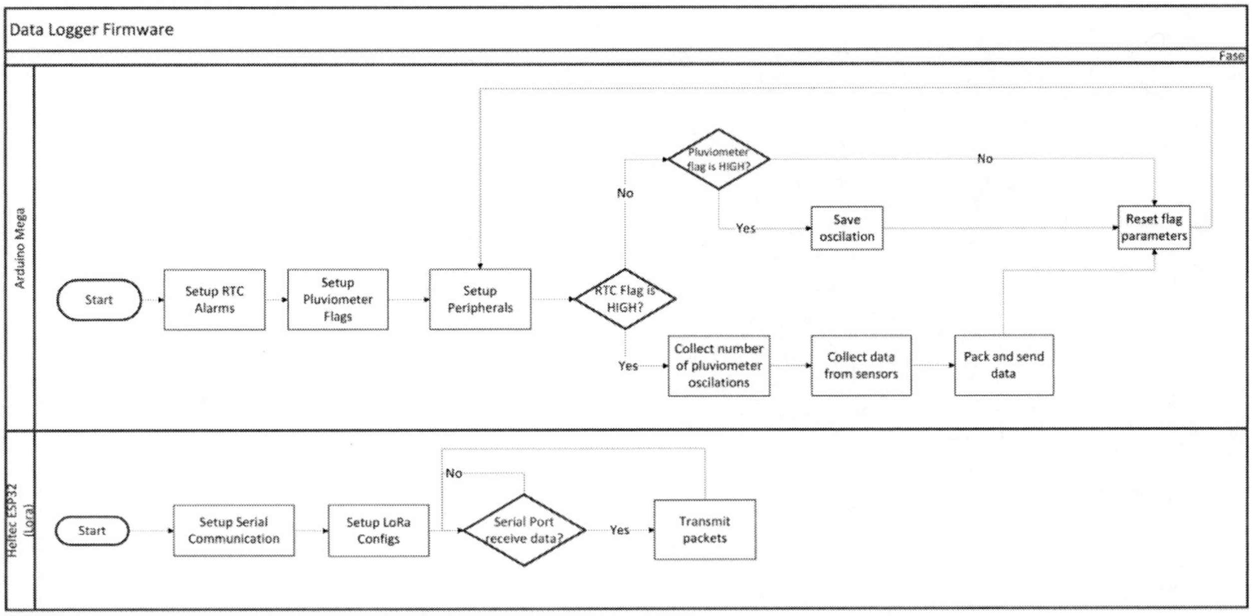


Figure 7. Data collection flowchart.

The receiving module was programmed to receive data permanently, unpack the received information, check the type of data, and transmit it to the correct ThingSpeak channel. Subsequently, it transmitted the necessary confirmation to the information sender station.

## III. Results and Discussion

The corn crop (*Zea mays.*) is divided into two major phases: vegetative and reproductive. Each vegetative stage is defined according to the last fully expanded leaf or out of the cartridge. The reproductive phases begin with mating and go on to physiological maturation, stage where the grains have a black layer at the insertion between the grain and the cob.

The growing stage of the maze crop, for the validation of this development, was defined into a period of time comprised between 60 and 65 days. Therefore, the complete monitoring time of climate and soil variables have took from 1440 hours to 1560 hours, since the night period also requires follow-up.

Thus, for the evaluation of the Lora wireless sensor network in a rural environment, wireless networks based on ZigBee (IEEE 802.15.4-based) and Wi-Fi (IEEE 802.11-based) were also tested for comparison purposes. Table I presents comparative information for these wireless network modalities.

In this context, the total energy consumption in kWh and the range distance in meters have been evaluated, as well as other parameters of interest. Therefore, for the maize cultivation monitoring time of 1560 hours a consumption of 0.16 kWh was observed for the platform based on LoRa, while using ZigBee and Wi-Fi a consumption of 0.40 kWh and 1.95 kWh respectively were observed, i.e., based on the use of a +5Vdc power supply for each of the technologies in order to calculate the amount of energy consumed during the same period of monitoring.

On the other hand, the range provided by the use of LoRa technology was observed to be 150 times superior to ZigBee and 60 times superior to Wi-Fi use.

The prototype was assembled using a breadboard (Figure 8) to validate the hardware and firmware in the laboratory before building the circuit boards and boxes for field application. During the tests, the collecting and receiving modules were placed 500 meters apart with a wall between them. There was no information loss in this distance according to the data from the memory card and the receiving log file. Eventually, some transmission and ThingSpeak failures occurred. Code improvements to allow resending and checking the Wi-Fi network were proposed to reduce failures.

Figure 9 shows a section of code configuring the use of a LoRa module in the Heltec Wi-Fi LoRa 32 board, specifically in the data receiving module. This configuration allows data exchange using both LoRa and Wi-Fi networks.

Table I
Main characteristics of the technologies ZigBee, Wi-Fi , and LoRa [26]–[28]

| **Indicator** | **Wireless Network's Technologies** | | |
|---|---|---|---|
| | **ZigBee** | **Wi-Fi** | **LoRa** |
| Range Average | up to 100m | up to 250m | up to 15 km |
| Power Consumption | 52 mA | 251mA | 20 mA |
| Baund Rate | up to 250 Kbps | 3 Mbps up to 866 Mbps | up to 50 Kbps |
| Robustness | High | Medium | High |
| Network topology | mesh | start, mesh | star-of-stars, mesh |

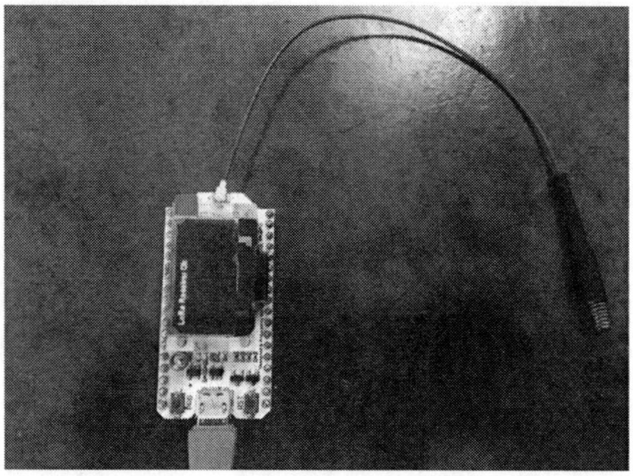

(a)

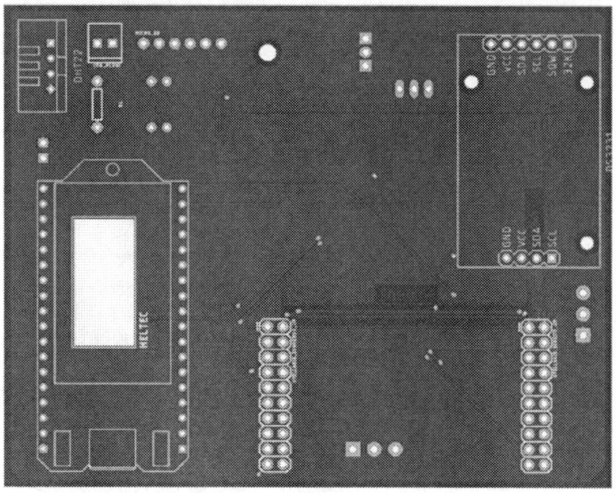

(b)

Figure 8. Prototypes for collecting and transmitting data through a LoRa network: (a) Network data receiver module; (b) Collector device board installed in the field.

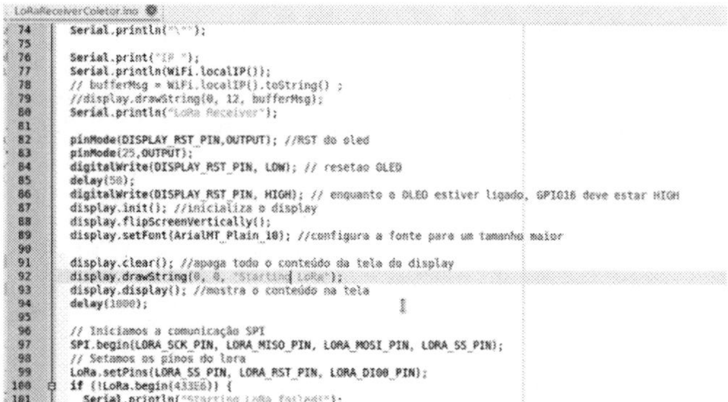

```
LoRaReceiverColetor.ino
Serial.println("\"");

Serial.print("IP ");
Serial.println(WiFi.localIP());
// bufferMsg = WiFi.localIP().toString() ;
//display.drawString(0, 12, bufferMsg);
Serial.println("LoRa Receiver");

pinMode(DISPLAY_RST_PIN,OUTPUT); //RST do oled
pinMode(25,OUTPUT);
digitalWrite(DISPLAY_RST_PIN, LOW); // resetao OLED
delay(50);
digitalWrite(DISPLAY_RST_PIN, HIGH); // enquanto o OLED estiver ligado, GPIO16 deve estar HIGH
display.init(); //inicializa o display
display.flipScreenVertically();
display.setFont(ArialMT_Plain_10); //configura a fonte para um tamanho maior

display.clear(); //apaga todo o conteúdo da tela do display
display.drawString(0, 0, "Starting LoRa");
display.display(); //mostra o conteúdo na tela
delay(1000);

// Iniciamos a comunicação SPI
SPI.begin(LORA_SCK_PIN, LORA_MISO_PIN, LORA_MOSI_PIN, LORA_SS_PIN);
// Setamos os pinos do lora
LoRa.setPins(LORA_SS_PIN, LORA_RST_PIN, LORA_DIO0_PIN);
if (!LoRa.begin(433E6)) {
  Serial.println("Starting LoRa failed!");
  while (1);
```

Figure 9. A section of the data receiving code.

Furthermore, experimental tests have allowed recording data into ThingSpeak, which can be analyzed using its tools. The charts in Figure 10 present an example for a period of 12 hours of data temporal series from both air humidity and air temperature in the agricultural area. Some data correctly transmitted using the LoRa network were not retransmitted to ThingSpeak.

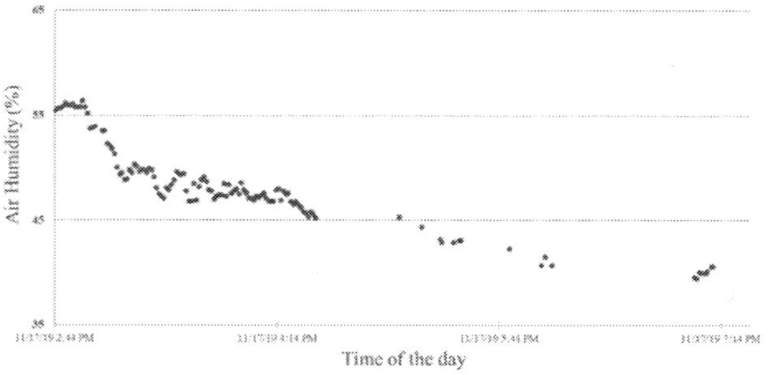


(a)

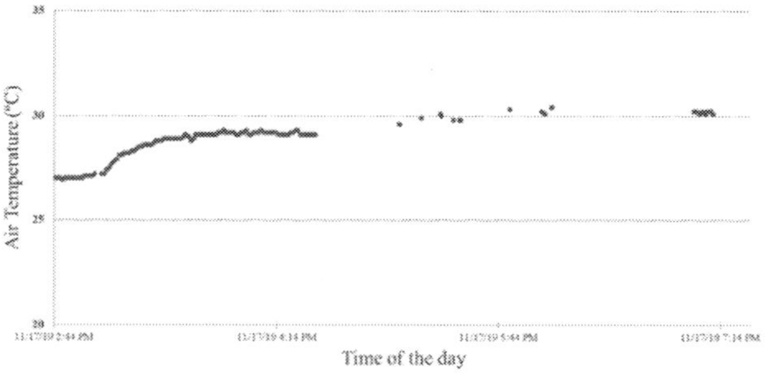


(b)

Figure 10. An example for a period of 12 hours of data temporal series from both air humidity (a), and air temperature (b) in the agricultural area. Such data are part of the variables set data vector for the evaluation of the soil quality analysis, which also uses the wind speed, rainfall, pH and the % of organic matter measurements from each plot.

During operation, it was observed that some data was not properly retransmitted. After verification, it was found the occurrence of interruption in the use of the Wi-Fi module due to the momentary unavailability of the Internet in the rural area. Once that such an occurrence has been verified, the algorithm has become reorganized for automatic reconnection to the network, i.e., when any events of this nature occur again. Also, energy saving concepts have been used based on deep-sleep, controlled by the ESP32 microcontroller present in the Heltec module, i.e., configuring the Real Time Clock (RTC) DS3231 to signal the moments when the microcontroller should actually work. The current consumption for the microcontroller's circuit when in deep-sleep are in the order of $20\mu A$ [29].

The contributions of this work involve the use of a long-range and low power consumption of agricultural data transmission that is very promising and suitable for application in the rural environment, mainly for agricultural management based on precision agriculture, which is an approach to farm management that uses information from sensors to ensure that crops and soil receive exactly what they need for optimum health and productivity.

Besides, based on such a concept it is possible to take into a better manner the risks that occurs in agricultural production, and their mitigation. However, to achieve this goal, so fundamental for production, it is necessary to monitor the behavior of soil, climate and plant variables, their values and ranges, as well as the dynamics for decision making in real time.

In this study, the risk modeling has referred to the risk on soil quality, one of the essential parts that make up the total agricultural risk.

Likewise, to establish the soil quality risk behavior, it is necessary to know the variability of air temperature and humidity, organic matter content, pH and availability of nutrients in the soil, among others. However, a merit function that can integrate either a set of variables or information about their behavior at instants of time has to be considered.

One way found to integrate the variables is the use of their occurrence probabilities obtained from the time series of the collected data, which are treated as random variables. In addition, using a risk model it is possible to meet prevention and containment strategies, so that as many scenarios as possible help the promotion of expected result in terms of number of tons/hectares.

## IV. Conclusions

In this present study it has been shown the use of LoRa wireless network for agricultural application, i.e., related to risk analysis. Results have shown that the whole implementations worked satisfactorily not only at the laboratory but also during the validation occurred in a corn's agricultural field. In such a context it has been observed that there are needs for some firmware corrections and additional agricultural experiments in order to increase system reliability to the users. Therefore, the use of a LoRa network has been proved to be suitable for agricultural application, with special interest for soil quality risk analysis.

In addition, another important aspect to be observed in these conclusions is that the development of a wireless sensor network based on Lora made it possible to transmit long range and operating agricultural data at low power consumption, which is promising for decision support in the rural environment.

Likewise, the development of the wireless network based on Lora minimized the limitations regarding the availability of energy sources and the difficulty of accessing the internet in rural areas, which required seeking customization for real-time operation considering variables of climate and soil which can bring impacts to soil quality during agricultural planting.

Future works will take into account the implementation of pH and organic-matter embedded smart sensors, as well as algorithms structured using Apache-Spark to operate the model for agricultural soil quality risk analysis.

## Acknowledgment

This study was financially supported by the São Paulo Research Foundation (FAPESP), process no. 17/19350-2, through an agreement involving IBM Brazil and the Brazilian Agricultural Research Corporation (Embrapa). The authors are also grateful for the institutional support by the Federal University of Mato Grosso (UFMT).

## References

[1] M. F. L. Pereira and P. E. Cruvinel, "Development of an automatic agricultural data collection system based on lora network and esp32 microprocessor (original in portuguese "desenvolvimento de um sistema de coleta automática dados agrícola baseado em rede lora e no microprocessador esp32" )," in *Anais da X Escola Regional de Informática de Mato Grosso*. SBC, 2019, pp. 43–48.

[2] A. Torre Neto and P. E. Cruvinel, "Use of microcontrollers and virtual reality in agriculture (original in portuguese: "uso de microcontroladores e realidade virtual na agricultura")," *Embrapa Instrumentação-Comunicado Técnico (INFOTECA-E)*, 1997.

[3] S. Monteleone *et al.*, "Exploring the adoption of precision agriculture for irrigation in the context of agriculture 4.0: The key role of internet of things," *Sensors*, vol. 20, no. 24, p. 7091, 2020.

[4] S. Navulur and M. G. Prasad, "Agricultural management through wireless sensors and internet of things," *International Journal of Electrical and Computer Engineering*, vol. 7, no. 6, p. 3492, 2017.

[5] P. E. Cruvinel, J. M. Naime, J. D. C. Pessoa, J. M. G. Beraldo, L. M. Rabello, and S. Crestana. (2017) Advanced digital tool for the agricultural risk management (original in portuguese: Ferramenta digital avançada para o gerenciamento de riscos agrícolas). [retrieved: June, 2021]. FAPESP - PITE. [Online]. Available: https://bv.fapesp.br/pt/auxilios/100768/ferramenta-digital-avancada-para-o-gerenciamento-de-riscos-agricolas/

[6] D. Karlen, S. Andrews, and J. Doran, "Soil quality: current concepts and applications," *Advances in Agronomy*, vol. 74, p. 40, 2001.

[7] V. P. Obade and R. Lal, "A standardized soil quality index for diverse field conditions," *Science of The Total Environment*, vol. 541, pp. 424–434, Jan. 2016.

[8] J. Paz-Ferreiro and S. Fu, "Biological indices for soil quality evaluation: perspectives and limitations," *Land Degradation & Development*, vol. 27, no. 1, pp. 14–25, 2016.

[9] E. K. Bünemann *et al.*, "Soil quality — a critical review," *Soil Biology and Biochemistry*, vol. 120, pp. 105–125, May 2018.

[10] W. Zhao, S. Lin, J. Han, R. Xu, and L. Hou, "Design and implementation of smart irrigation system based on LoRa," in *2017 IEEE Globecom Workshops (GC Wkshps)*. IEEE, dec 2017.

[11] M. S. Mekala and P. Viswanathan, "A survey: Smart agriculture IoT with cloud computing," in *2017 International conference on Microelectronic Devices, Circuits and Systems (ICMDCS)*. IEEE, aug 2017.

[12] C. Pham, A. Rahim, and P. Cousin, "Low-cost, long-range open IoT for smarter rural african villages," in *2016 IEEE International Smart Cities Conference (ISC2)*. IEEE, sep 2016.

[13] H. Automation, "Wifi lora 32," Disponível em https://heltec.org/project/wifi-lora-32/, 2019.

[14] M. Zaharia, R. S. Xin, P. Wendell, T. Das, M. Armbrust, A. Dave, X. Meng, J. Rosen, S. Venkataraman, M. J. Franklin, A. Ghodsi, J. Gonzalez, S. Shenker, and I. Stoica, "Apache Spark: A Unified Engine for Big Data Processing," *Commun. ACM*, vol. 59, no. 11, pp. 56–65, 2016. [Online]. Available: http://doi.acm.org/10.1145/2934664

[15] J. C. Boechat, M. F. L. Pereira, and O. M. Dantas, "Low cost rain gauge for rain data collection and wireless transmission using the mqtt protocol (original in portuguese: Pluviógrafo de baixo custo para coleta e transmissão sem fio de dados de chuva, usando o protocolo mqtt," in *Anais da IX Escola Regional de Informática de Mato Grosso*, Barra do Bugres, Nov. 2018, pp. 48–57.

[16] U. Raza, P. Kulkarni, and M. Sooriyabandara, "Low power wide area networks: An overview," *IEEE Communications Surveys & Tutorials*, vol. 19, no. 2, pp. 855–873, 2017.

[17] J. P. Queralta, T. N. Gia, Z. Zou, H. Tenhunen, and T. Westerlund, "Comparative study of lpwan technologies on unlicensed bands for m2m communication in the iot: Beyond lora and lorawan," *Procedia Computer Science*, vol. 155, pp. 343–350, 2019.

[18] B. Nunes, "Introdução a lora, nb-iot e sigfox," Disponível online em https://www.embarcados.com.br/lora-nb-iot-e-sigfox/, 2017.

[19] B. Miles, E.-B. Bourennane, S. Boucherkha, and S. Chikhi, "A study of lorawan protocol performance for iot applications in smart agriculture," *Computer Communications*, vol. 164, pp. 148–157, 2020. [Online]. Available: https://www.sciencedirect.com/science/article/pii/S0140366420319575

[20] I. Butun, N. Pereira, and M. Gidlund, "Security risk analysis of lorawan and future directions," *Future Internet*, vol. 11, no. 1, 2019. [Online]. Available: https://www.mdpi.com/1999-5903/11/1/3

[21] G. Codeluppi, A. Cilfone, L. Davoli, and G. Ferrari, "Lorafarm: A lorawan-based smart farming modular iot architecture," *Sensors*, vol. 20, no. 7, 2020. [Online]. Available: https://www.mdpi.com/1424-8220/20/7/2028

[22] R. K. Singh, M. Aernouts, M. De Meyer, M. Weyn, and R. Berkvens, "Leveraging lorawan technology for precision agriculture in greenhouses," *Sensors*, vol. 20, no. 7, 2020. [Online]. Available: https://www.mdpi.com/1424-8220/20/7/1827

[23] N. Sornin, M. Luis, T. Eirich, T. Kramp, and O. Hersent, "Lora wan technical specification," *LoRA Alliance Version 1.0*, pp. 1–82, 2015.

[24] Espressif, "Esp32 series datasheet," Disponível online em "https://www.espressif.com/sites/default/files/documentation/esp32_datasheet_en.pdf", Espressif Systems, 2019.

[25] T. Hareendran, "A review of the mini sx1278 lora transceiver module," Disponível em https://www.electroschematics.com/14383/rf-radio-frequency/, Julho 2019.

[26] A. Mahmood, N. Javaid, and S. Razzaq, "A review of wireless communications for smart grid," *Renewable and Sustainable Energy Reviews*, vol. 41, pp. 248–260, 2015. [Online]. Available: https://www.sciencedirect.com/science/article/pii/S1364032114007126

[27] H. Alobaidy, J. Mandeep, R. Nordin, and N. F. Abdullah, "A review on zigbee based wsns: Concepts infrastructure applications and challenges," *Int. J. Electr. Electron. Eng. Telecommun.*, vol. 9, no. 3, pp. 189–198, 2020.

[28] M. Botella-Campos, L. Parra, S. Sendra, and J. Lloret, "Wlan ieee 802.11b/g/n coverage study for rural areas," in *2020 International Conference on Control, Automation and Diagnosis (ICCAD)*, 2020, pp. 1–6.

[29] J. Boechat, O. M. Dantas, and M. F. L. Pereira, "Automatic climate data collector using wireless networks and mqtt protocol in data transmission (original in portuguese "coletor automático de dados climáticos utilizando redes sem fio e o protocolo mqtt na transmissão de dados")," in *Anais do XII Congresso Brasileiro de Agroinformática - IoT na Agricultura*. SBIAGRO, 2019, p. 2.

# Combining Multiple Modalities with Perceiver in Imitation-based Urban Driving

Shubham Juneja
Institute of Data Science &
Digital Technologies
Vilnius University
Vilnius, Lithuania
Email: shubham.juneja@mif.stud.vu.lt

Virginijus Marcinkevičius
Institute of Data Science &
Digital Technologies
Vilnius University
Vilnius, Lithuania
Email: virginijus.marcinkevicius@mif.vu.lt

Povilas Daniušis
Department of Business
Technologies & Entrepreneurship
Vilnius Gediminas Technical University
Vilnius, Lithuania
Email: povilas.daniusis@vgtu.lt

***Abstract*—Traditional autonomous driving methods have relied on multiple sensor inputs for their success in decision making. Meanwhile, these methods require greater engineering effort as they consist of multiple modules than end-to-end methods which learn from data. In comparison, end-to-end methods rely on only a single modality and lack the ability to thoroughly generalise to new environments compared to traditional approaches. To enhance the current state-of-the-art methods, we propose using additional environmental information into an end-to-end learned method by employing the Perceiver architecture. The proposed technique aims to use more than one modality by fusing sensor data into a learner to generalise better in urban environments.**

***Keywords*—*imitation learning; urban driving; perceiver.***

## I. INTRODUCTION

With the rise in popularity and demand for autonomy, research on autonomous driving has been at the forefront. The methods from the field not only contribute to transportation but also to the area of robotics [1]. While being vital to more than one industry, the task of driving autonomously in urban environments remains in the phase of research due to the high complexity of the problem and issues it faces, such as difficulties in generalising to unseen environments.

The current state-of-the-art autonomous driving systems are either based on the traditional autonomous vehicle pipelines using a modular approach where the system is divided into modules with multiple sensors and algorithms [2] or based on approaches that learn driving end-to-end directly from data [3]–[5]. Modular approaches leverage the presence of multiple sensors by fusing information to capture various characteristics from the surrounding and have been approaching human-level performance (e.g. Tesla Autopilot system) [6]. Meanwhile, they suffer in terms of the engineering effort required to tune each of the modules. In comparison, end-to-end learned methods thrive on requiring barely any tuning but prominently depend on a single front-facing camera for sensor input. This trend is dominant across recent end-to-end learning techniques, be it imitation learning or reinforcement learning, along with the disadvantage of showing generalisation to new environments to be a complex problem.

With 2D image data being the primary modality in end-to-end techniques [3]–[5][7], recent methods leverage convolutional neural networks (CNNs) as a candidate learner, which introduces a prerequisite of additional modifications to the architecture when involving different input configurations [8][9]. The recently proposed Perceiver architecture [10] attempts on employing different input data modalities into a single architecture. It is designed to work with arbitrary input configurations of different modalities and to efficiently handle high dimensional inputs. Various research results have shown the advantage of such data fusion across systems [6][11].

Considering the limitations of the current state-of-the-art, we make the contribution of proposing to fuse the front-facing camera data with an additional perception stream (using a LIDAR sensor) into a learner based on Perceiver architecture to learn the skill of urban driving using imitation learning. Further, we propose evaluating the learned method with the CARLA [12] and NoCrash [13] benchmarks.

The rest of the paper is organised as follows. Section II describes literature concerning urban driving and learning methods in the area; section III describes the proposed approach and the incipient implementation details; section IV concludes this idea paper.

## II. RELATED WORK

End-to-end urban driving methods, be it based on imitation learning or reinforcement learning, have been relying on 2D images for making driving decisions, which can be mainly due to the rich data images provide [6]. Conditional affordance learning [14] is a recent method which predicts the affordances with the use of a CNN from images on a vehicle and learns to drive with the use of imitation learning. Methods such as affordance based reinforcement learning [3] and implicit affordances learning [5], attempt to do a similar job but use reinforcement learning as the learning method. Learning by cheating method [4] uses a CNN to project feature maps from which it learns to drive using imitation learning. However, the hardware used on vehicles is capable of having more than one sensor to provide rich data. There are also methods which use some speed measurement along with image data [7][13]. Though this data might not be rich and it is integrated by the method of concatenation, the technique may not promise to utilise the data in the selected deep learning architecture.

The Perceiver architecture is capable of working with arbitrary configurations of inputs by using multiple transformer units. Also, Perceiver's inputs can be from different modalities, and the architecture does not require modifications, as opposed to CNNs, which require architectural adjustments. The architecture proves to be capable of dealing with large

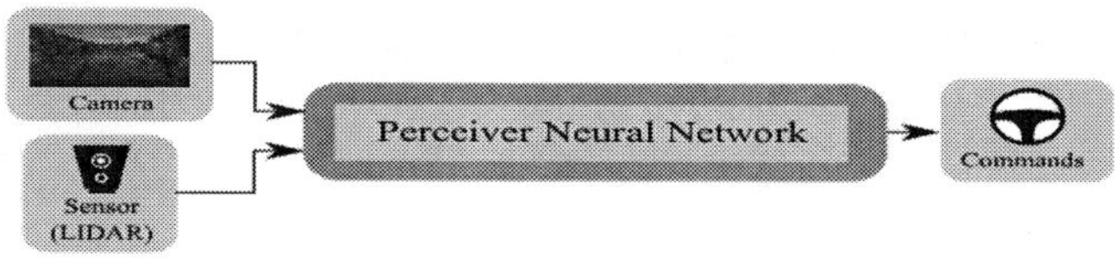


Fig. 1. Overview of the proposed method.

size and multimodal data format at once, and hence shows the capacity to be suitable to deal with images along with LIDAR data.

Reinforcement learning methods applied to the problem of driving in urban areas are quite a recent success and have only displayed results in simulated environments [3][5]. This leaves out a question if it is possible to hold up the skill level when deployed in the real world. In contrast, imitation learning methods have a long history of being applied in real world environments [7][15][16]. This motivates us to lean towards imitation learning rather than reinforcement learning.

## III. Method and experiments

### A. Approach

Our approach is to learn the skill of urban driving through observing two sensors in order to take advantage of data fusion, as shown in Figure 1. We plan to do so with the Perceiver architecture instead of a CNN, as the Perceiver architecture does not need any modifications to integrate multiple modalities into a single learner. For input sensors, we initially plan the use of a camera and a LIDAR sensor as such sensors show the capability of capturing rich environmental information and are widely used in autonomous navigation research.

### B. Environment and Benchmarks

For the environment, we choose the CARLA simulator[12] over other possible options as it makes it simpler to compare results to the state-of-the-art methods since the widely used benchmarks in the area of urban driving research, i.e. NoCrash and CARLA benchmarks, rely on this simulation environment. And hence we plan to use the mentioned benchmarks to compare our results.

### C. Implementation plan

We aim to train a neural network with the architecture of a Perceiver to classify sensor inputs into discrete control commands. For which, we plan to collect data from the selected two sensors along with corresponding control commands to fully capture expert demonstrations. Additionally, during optimisation of the learner, we plan to use augmentation methods which randomly distort sensor data from either of the sensors or possibly both sensors to an extent, to help with regularisation across modalities. Furthermore, if necessary, additional data can be collected using the DAgger algorithm [17].

This methods and experiments plan is empirically bound to changes and improvements as the proposed method is in an incipient stage.

## IV. Conclusion

Our work proposes a step towards utilising multiple modalities in imitation learning for urban driving methods. The idea of fusing sensory information could exploit the complementary characteristics of each sensor involved. Moreover, in situations where one of the sensors might be blinded, another one can assist in decision making and hence improving the overall performance.

## References

[1] P. Daniušis, S. Juneja, L. Valatka, and L. Petkevičius, "Topological navigation graph framework," *Autonomous Robots*, May 2021. [Online]. Available: https://doi.org/10.1007/s10514-021-09980-x

[2] J. Ziegler *et al.*, "Making bertha drive—an autonomous journey on a historic route," *IEEE Intelligent transportation systems magazine*, vol. 6, no. 2, pp. 8–20, 2014.

[3] T. Agarwal, H. Arora, and J. Schneider, "Affordance-based reinforcement learning for urban driving," *arXiv preprint arXiv:2101.05970*, 2021.

[4] D. Chen, B. Zhou, V. Koltun, and P. Krähenbühl, "Learning by cheating," in *Conference on Robot Learning*. PMLR, 2020, pp. 66–75.

[5] M. Toromanoff, E. Wirbel, and F. Moutarde, "End-to-end model-free reinforcement learning for urban driving using implicit affordances," in *Proceedings of the IEEE/CVF Conference on Computer Vision and Pattern Recognition*, 2020, pp. 7153–7162.

[6] J. Janai, F. Güney, A. Behl, and A. Geiger, "Computer vision for autonomous vehicles: Problems, datasets and state of the art," *Foundations and Trends® in Computer Graphics and Vision*, vol. 12, no. 1–3, pp. 1–308, 2020. [Online]. Available: http://dx.doi.org/10.1561/0600000079

[7] F. Codevilla, M. Müller, A. López, V. Koltun, and A. Dosovitskiy, "End-to-end driving via conditional imitation learning," in *2018 IEEE International Conference on Robotics and Automation (ICRA)*. IEEE, 2018, pp. 4693–4700.

[8] A. Karpathy *et al.*, "Large-scale video classification with convolutional neural networks," in *Proceedings of the IEEE conference on Computer Vision and Pattern Recognition*, 2014, pp. 1725–1732.

[9] A. Karpathy and L. Fei-Fei, "Deep visual-semantic alignments for generating image descriptions," in *Proceedings of the IEEE conference on computer vision and pattern recognition*, 2015, pp. 3128–3137.

[10] A. Jaegle *et al.*, "Perceiver: General perception with iterative attention," *CoRR*, vol. abs/2103.03206, 2021. [Online]. Available: https://arxiv.org/abs/2103.03206

[11] F. Nobis, M. Geisslinger, M. Weber, J. Betz, and M. Lienkamp, "A deep learning-based radar and camera sensor fusion architecture for object detection," in *2019 Sensor Data Fusion: Trends, Solutions, Applications (SDF)*, 2019, pp. 1–7.

[12] A. Dosovitskiy, G. Ros, F. Codevilla, A. Lopez, and V. Koltun, "Carla: An open urban driving simulator," in *Conference on robot learning*. PMLR, 2017, pp. 1–16.

[13] F. Codevilla, E. Santana, A. M. López, and A. Gaidon, "Exploring the limitations of behavior cloning for autonomous driving," in *Proceedings of the IEEE/CVF International Conference on Computer Vision*, 2019, pp. 9329–9338.

[14] A. Sauer, N. Savinov, and A. Geiger, "Conditional affordance learning for driving in urban environments," in *Conference on Robot Learning*. PMLR, 2018, pp. 237–252.

[15] D. A. Pomerleau, "Alvinn: An autonomous land vehicle in a neural network," in *Proceedings of the 1st International Conference on Neural Information Processing Systems*, ser. NIPS'88. Cambridge, MA, USA: MIT Press, 1988, p. 305–313.

[16] M. Bojarski *et al.*, "End to end learning for self-driving cars," *CoRR*, vol. abs/1604.07316, 2016. [Online]. Available: http://arxiv.org/abs/1604.07316

[17] S. Ross, G. J. Gordon, and J. Andrew Bagnell, "A reduction of imitation learning and structured prediction to no-regret online learning," *J. Mach. Learn. Res.*, vol. 15, pp. 627–635, 11 2010.

# Design of Surface Acoustic Wave Motors With Non-piezoelectric Stator Material

Richard Günther, René Richter and Jens Lienig
*Institute of Electromechanical and Electronic Design*
*Dresden University of Technology*
Dresden, Germany
Email: richard.guenther@tu-dresden.de, rene.richter@tu-dresden.de and jens@ieee.org

***Abstract*—Surface Acoustic Wave (SAW) motors are specific piezoelectric motors that use traveling waves instead of the stator's natural vibration. Despite their promising potential due to their high blocking forces, high positioning accuracy and simple design, practical applications of these novel motors are still missing. Hence, we present guidelines for designing such an SAW motor. By focusing on a non-piezoelectric stator material, a wide range of stator materials can potentially be used. First, we introduce the structure of a Finite Element Method (FEM) analysis, which allows for the application and design of piezoelectric units. Furthermore, a numerical motor model is described, which calculates characteristics of such a motor. The focus is on expansions, considering the dynamic losses of the motor, as well as roughness and flatness of its contact surfaces. Our findings allow the design and improvement of SAW motors with non-piezoelectric stator material, thus contributing to their first practical application.**

***Index Terms*—piezoelectric motor, ultrasonic motor, SAW motor, Rayleigh waves, PZT**

## I. Introduction

The availability of increasingly favorable and more compact control technologies allows the use of actuators with complex controls and the numerous use of small drives in general. Thus, there is – aside from a more frequented use of electronic commutated electromagnetic motors – a wide range of novel piezoelectric motors presented in the literature [1]–[5]. A special type of piezoelectric motor is the Surface Acoustic Wave (SAW) motor, which uses traveling waves instead of the stator's natural vibration [6]. Due to the high operation frequency it yields a very high power density and allows for powerful miniaturized linear motors. The latter are used for mirror adjusters in industrial sector or autofocus functionality in consumer lenses. When the SAW travels over the stator's surface, each point of the surface oscillates elliptically. According to Fig. 1, this behavior allows for a relative motion between the stator and the slider, which is pressed onto the stator. Cylindrical projections on the slider's contact surface increase the contact pressure to remove air between stator and slider. The stator is made from $LiNbO_3$. Hence, SAW can easily be generated by Inter-Digital Transducers (IDT). However, designers are restricted to a relatively expensive brittle single crystal with this setup. In contrast, an SAW motor with non-piezoelectric stator material allows for a wide range of stator materials. Previously, we built an SAW motor with a $3\,\mathrm{mm}$ thick stator made from steel type 1.4016 and presented

Fig. 1. Functional principle of a SAW motor: SAW travels on stator (orange) and causes a relative motion of the slider (yellow)

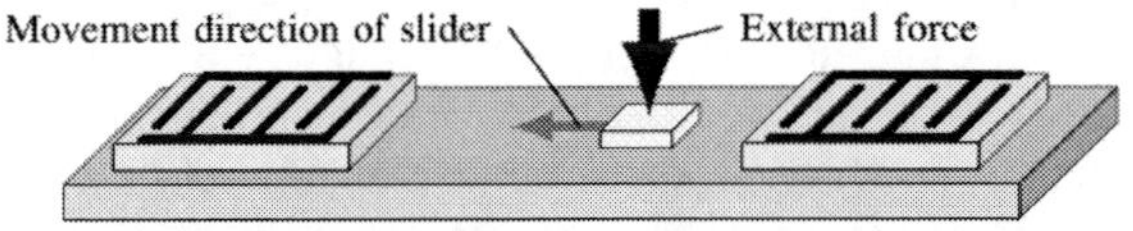


Fig. 2. Basic construction of SAW motor with non-piezoelectric stator material: Piezoelectric unit (orange block) generates SAW (orange arrow) on non-piezoelectric substrate (grey); Pressed slider (yellow) moves towards active piezoelectric unit

exemplary measurements of the motor characteristics in [7]. For SAW generation, normal polarized piezoelectric units with a thickness of $200\,\mu\mathrm{m}$ are adhered onto the roughened non-piezoelectric stator by epoxy resin as illustrated in Fig. 2. These units are made from the material *Sonox® P53* and are excited by IDTs with 30 finger pairs and a doubled finger spacing of $\lambda_f = 800\,\mu\mathrm{m}$. The silicon slider has 16 560 projections with a diameter of $22.5\,\mu\mathrm{m}$ and a similar setup as the slider, described in [6]. The motor achieved a blocking force of $0.19\,\mathrm{N}$ and an idling speed of $29\,\mathrm{mm\,s^{-1}}$ for a normal frequency of $3.85\,\mathrm{MHz}$ and an applied voltage amplitude of $50\,\mathrm{V}$. Furthermore, we presented Finite Element Method (FEM) models for the characterization of the piezoelectric units [7]. A modified numerical motor model that calculates motor characteristics starting from a given SAW based on [8] was used for motor characterization.

Despite our aforementioned findings in [7], practical implementations of these motors are still missing. Hence, the contribution of this paper is to present verified guidelines for designing such an SAW motor with non-piezoelectric stator material. Section II explains necessary FEM models and an improved numerical motor model in detail. Based on this, Section III presents our derived guidelines, which

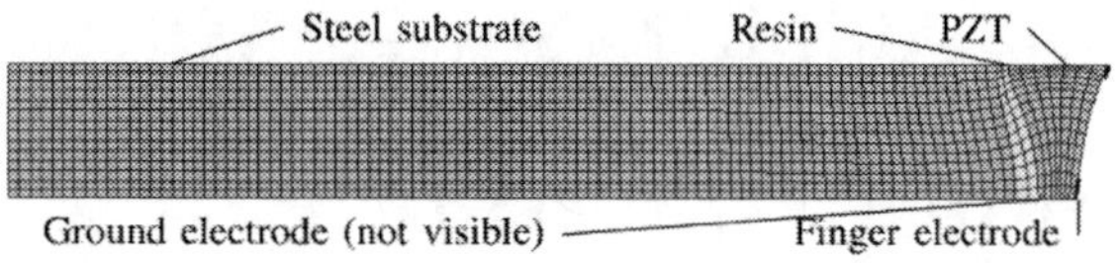


Fig. 3. FEM model for modal analysis of SAW generating unit on steel substrate

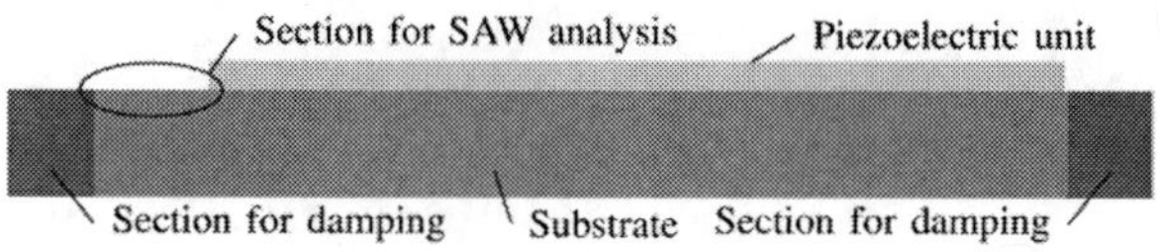


Fig. 4. Basic structure of transient FEM model

allow the design and implementation of advanced motors and thus support future applications of this new actuator principle. Finally, Section IV summarizes the importance of the presented guidelines for future works.

## II. Numerical Models

### A. Finite element models

Our two-dimensional FEM models consider the elasticity matrix, piezoelectric constants, permittivity and density for the piezoelectric material. The remaining materials are defined by *Young's* modulus, *Poisson's* ratio and density.

*1) Modal analysis:* According to Fig. 3, the first model takes into account only a section with the length of one finger spacing $\lambda_f/2$. With the constraint of preventing translation in the direction of propagation at boundary, it describes a stator and piezoelectric unit with infinite length. It can be used for modal analyses to determine the approximate working frequency $f$, which depends on the thickness of piezoelectric unit. The element size is $\lambda_f/18 \times \lambda_f/18$. It is important to set the piezoelectric constants to zero, because at resonance the power supply provides the displacement current for the actuator.

*2) Transient analysis:* A second model describes the whole piezoelectric unit, followed by a section with exposed stator material and a section with strong damping at each side as shown in Fig. 4. Thus, we can describe a realistic excitation of the piezoelectric unit and study the traveling SAW. The damped sections avoid a standing SAW due to reflections at the edges. The element size is $\lambda_f/25 \times \lambda_f/25$ at the top surface and increases to $\lambda_f/25 \times \lambda_f/2.5$ at the bottom due to a smaller calculation time. The time step size is $1/40f$.

For excitation of the piezoelectric unit, a sinusoidal voltage with the amplitude $\hat{U}$ is applied at the IDT. A displacement due to the SAW can be observed. Furthermore, we can read out the amplitude $\hat{q}$ and phase $\phi_q$ of the electric charge $q$ of the piezoelectric unit. This allows us to determine the electric impedance $Z$:

$$Z = \frac{\hat{U}}{2\pi f \hat{q}} \mathrm{e}^{-\mathrm{i}\left(\phi_q + \frac{\pi}{2}\right)}. \tag{1}$$

If the dielectric loss $\tan\delta$ is significant, it can be considered as follows:

$$Z_{\tan\delta} = \Re(Z) + \tan\delta\,|\Im(Z)| + \mathrm{i}\Im(Z). \tag{2}$$

The impedance curves of the stator, presented in [7], are shown in Fig. 5. The higher amounts of impedance at resonances are noteworthy. The distinctive resonance of the simulation model is based on the absence of tolerances. The

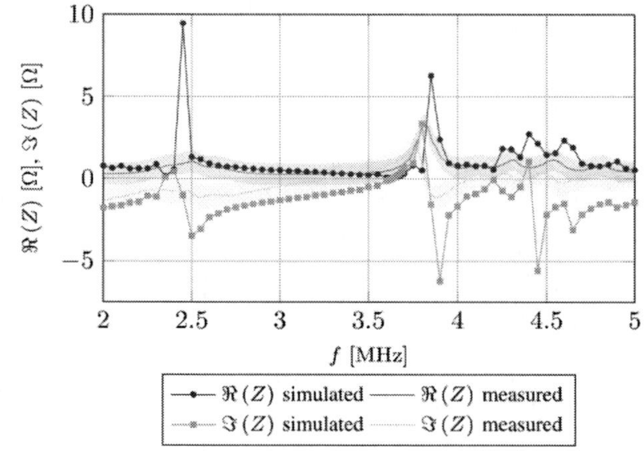


Fig. 5. Frequency dependent simulated and measured impedances for stator made from non-piezoelectric material; Measurement uncertainty is displayed transparently [7]

resonance frequencies are slightly shifted due to material and manufacturing deviations. The simulated normal displacement of stator's surface is $5487\,\mathrm{pm\,V^{-1}}$ at a frequency of $3.63\,\mathrm{MHz}$. This displacement is 17 times higher than the according measurement, with $(314 \pm 76)\,\mathrm{pm\,V^{-1}}$ at a frequency of $3.80\,\mathrm{MHz}$ [7]. The large difference can be explained by the smaller real part of the impedance for resonance with $\Re(Z(3.63\,\mathrm{MHz})) = 45.0\,\mathrm{m\Omega}$, according to Fig. 5, compared to the measured resistance of $\Re(Z(3.80\,\mathrm{MHz})) = 3.17\,\Omega$. Consequently, there is a smaller difference between simulated and measured SAW power. While the simulated efficiency is $30\,\%$, the measurement shows an efficiency of $(16.9 \pm 9.7)\,\%$. For calculation of efficiencies, the SAW power can be derived from displacement equations of *Rayleigh* waves [9] and by the definition of electric power:

$$P_{el} = 0.5\Re(S_{el}) = 0.5\Re\left(\frac{u^2}{Z}\right) = 0.5\Re\left(\frac{\hat{U}^2}{2Z}\right). \tag{3}$$

Here, $S_{el}$ and $u$ are the complex electric power and voltage, respectively. The factor 0.5 results from the fact that two SAW were generated by the piezoelectric unit.

### B. Numerical motor model

Our numerical motor model is based on an existing model presented in [8], which considers the contact between one projection and the stator. This contact is described by normal and tangential stiffnesses of the slider $K_{sl\,n}$ and $K_{sl\,t}$ and the stator $K_{st\,n}$ and $K_{st\,t}$, respectively, as shown in Fig. 6. The stator's normal and tangential displacements $d_{st\,n}(t)$ and

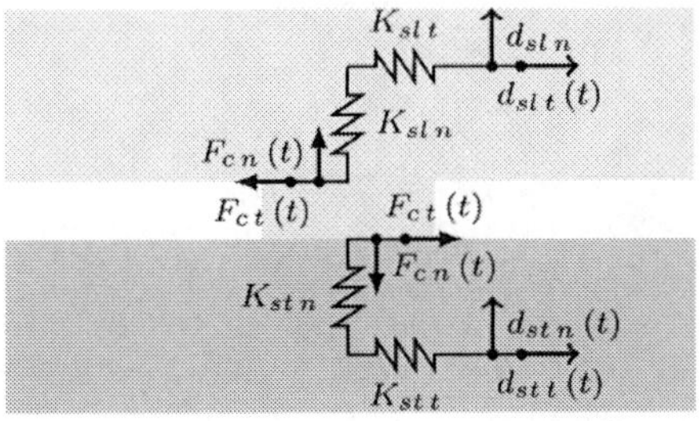


Fig. 6. Contact mechanics at one projection, used for the numeric motor model

$d_{st\,t}\,(t)$, respectively, are given by the SAW. Furthermore, we can define a normal offset $d_{sl\,n}$ of the slider. We can observe a phase with contact and a phase without contact within one period. When there is contact, the tangential force $F_{c\,t}\,(t)$ cannot exceed the normal force $F_{c\,n}\,(t)$ multiplied with the friction coefficient. If the tangential force is smaller, we notice sticking. If it is bigger, the force is limited and we notice slipping. The average force over one period equals the feed force of the considered projection. Defining a time dependent tangential slider displacement $d_{sl\,t}\,(t)$, we can consider different points of the motor characteristic. Considering all projections in a line orthogonal to the direction of SAW propagation, we can multiply the feed force by the number of projections in a line. Furthermore, it is possible to determine the friction power of the projection line and substract it from the initial SAW power. The equations for *Rayleigh* waves [9] allow for determining the new SAW amplitude at the next projection line. This procedure is repeated until all projections of the slider have been considered. Thus, the motor model is able to calculate velocity-force-diagrams. The input parameters are the density and elastic behavior of the contact materials, the normal force, the friction coefficient, the geometry and number of projections, and the frequency and amplitude of SAW. The model shows a positive influence of a high number of projections on the motor characteristic while maintaining the overall contact surface [14]. Furthermore, high friction coefficients and *Young's* moduli improve the motor's behavior.

This initial model uses an effective factor of $0.6$. This means, in one direction only $60\,\%$ of the projections will contact the stator. Considering both directions, only $36\,\%$ of all projections will be used. A logical explanation for that factor would be the roughness and flatness of stator and slider. However, in this case the factor should be dependent on the pressing force. As roughness and flatness are important parameters for motors with a polycrystalline stator, the motor model was expanded by a realistic definition of the effective factor in [7]. If the slider is placed over the stator without contacting it, we could determine a distance for each projection towards the stator. Shifting the slider towards the stator, we observe a contact force when the first projection is contacted. Progressively more projections get in contact and their contact forces will be added up. For a large amount of projections and normal distributed projection distances, the total contact force can be described as follows:

$$F_N = n_{pr} K_{ov\,n} \int_{-\infty}^{d_{sl\,n}} N\left(d_n, R_a\right)\, dd_n \tag{4}$$

where $n_{pr}$ is the number of all slider's projections and $K_{ov\,n}$ is the combined normal stiffness of slider and stator for one projection. The value $N\left(d_n, R_a\right)$ is the cumulative distribution function of the distances, $d_n$ the current displacement of the slider, $R_a$ the average roughness value and $d_{sl\,n}$ the slider displacement for the sought contact force. Therefore, the motor model integrates iteratively until the sought force is reached. Then the roughness dependent effective factor is given by:

$$\eta_{ro} = \sqrt{N\left(d_{sl\,n}, R_a\right)}. \tag{5}$$

Often the flatness can be described by a spherical shape, where the corresponding distances are not normally distributed. In this case, we can determine the amount of contacted projections by *Hertzian* contact theory. For a given sphere radius $R_{sp}$, the contact radius $R_c$ can be calculated as follows [10]:

$$R_c = \sqrt[3]{\frac{3F_N R_{sp}}{4D^\star}}, \tag{6}$$

$$\text{with } \frac{1}{D^\star} = \frac{1-\nu_{st}^2}{D_{st}} + \frac{1-\nu_{sl}^2}{D_{sl}}.$$

Here, $D_{sl}$ and $D_{st}$ are the Young's moduli of the slider and the stator, respectively, and $\nu_{sl}$ and $\nu_{st}$ are the Poisson's ratios of the slider and the stator, respectively. Using this contact radius, the flatness effective factor can be determined as follows:

$$\eta_{fl} = \sqrt{\frac{\pi R_c^2}{b_{sl}^2}} = \frac{\sqrt{\pi}}{b_{sl}} \sqrt[3]{\frac{3F_N R_{sp}}{4D^\star}} \tag{7}$$

where $b_{sl}$ is the edge length of the quadratic slider. Finally, the overall effective factor is given by:

$$\eta = \eta_{ro} \cdot \eta_{fl}. \tag{8}$$

Fig. 7 shows calculated motor characteristics for several spherical elevations and roughnesses for the mentioned SAW motor with non-piezoelectric stator material, a normal SAW amplitude of $3\,\mathrm{nm}$ at the surface, and an overall contact force of $4\,\mathrm{N}$. We can see that the flatness of $33\,\mathrm{nm}$ for the slider length of $4\,\mathrm{mm}$, which is feasible by lapping, is uncritical. However, we observe that the attainable roughness of $4.4\,\mathrm{nm}$ on the used steel downgrades the motor characteristic.

In addition, we expand the existing motor model by considering dynamic losses. Discrete *Fourier* transform allows to calculate the power of a bandlimited signal [11]. Thus, the periodic contact force curves can be decompositioned into

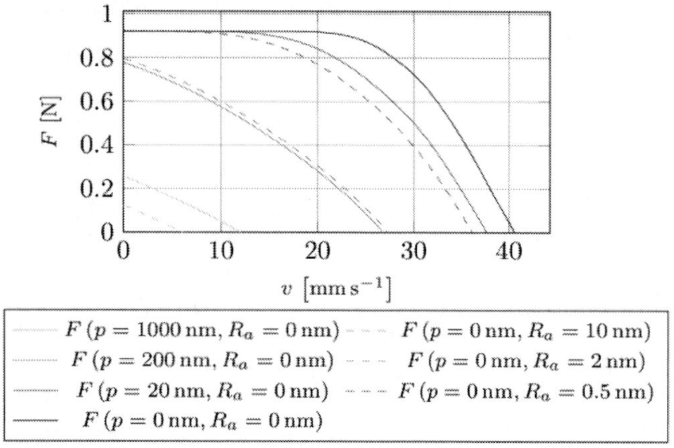


Fig. 7. Motor characteristics by motor model depending on varying spherical elevations $p$ and average roughness values $R_a$; Motor as described in [7] with a normal SAW amplitude of 3 nm at the surface and an overall contact force of 4 N

harmonic forces $F_f$ by discrete *Fourier* transform of $O$-th order [12]:

$$
\begin{aligned}
F_f =& g_0 + \sum_{j=1}^{O} \left(g_j \cos 2\pi f j t + o_j \sin 2\pi f j t\right), \\
\text{with } g_j =& \frac{2 \sin \frac{\pi j}{n_p}}{\pi j} \sum_{m=0}^{n_p-1} \left(F_m \cos \frac{2\pi j m}{n_p}\right) \\
\text{and } o_j =& \frac{2 \sin \frac{\pi j}{n_p}}{\pi j} \sum_{m=0}^{n_p-1} \left(F_m \sin \frac{2\pi j m}{n_p}\right)
\end{aligned}
\tag{9}
$$

where $g_j$ and $o_j$ are the $j$-th *Fourier* coefficients for even and odd functions, respectively. The value $F_m$ is the force at the discrete point $m$ and $n_p$ is the number of discrete points for one period. For normal and tangential harmonic excitations of circular regions on an elastic half space the mechanical impedances $Z_{M\,n}$ and $Z_{M\,t}$, respectively, can be described as follows [13]:

$$
\begin{aligned}
Z_{M\,n} =& \frac{4\mu R_p}{2\pi f (1-\nu)} \left(B_{n\,2\,1}\xi + B_{n\,2\,2}\xi^3 + \mathrm{i}\left(B_{t\,1\,1}\xi^2 - 1\right)\right), \\
Z_{M\,t} =& \frac{4\mu R_p}{2\pi f \left(1-\frac{\nu}{2}\right)} \left(B_{t\,2\,1} - B_{t\,2\,2}\xi^3 + \mathrm{i}\left(B_{t\,1\,1}\xi^2 - 1\right)\right) \\
& \text{with } \xi = \frac{2\pi f R_p}{c_T} < 0.7.
\end{aligned}
\tag{10}
$$

Here, $\mu$ is the second *Lamé* constant, $R_p$ is the projection radius and $B_{n\,j\,m}$ and $B_{t\,j\,m}$ are numerically determined coefficients for normal and tangential direction, respectively. The value $c_T$ describes the transversal wave velocity. For a mechanical impedance, the dynamic power loss can be determined as follows:

$$
P_\mathrm{d} = \Re\left(\frac{\hat{F}_j^{\,2}}{2 Z_\mathrm{M}}\right). \tag{11}
$$

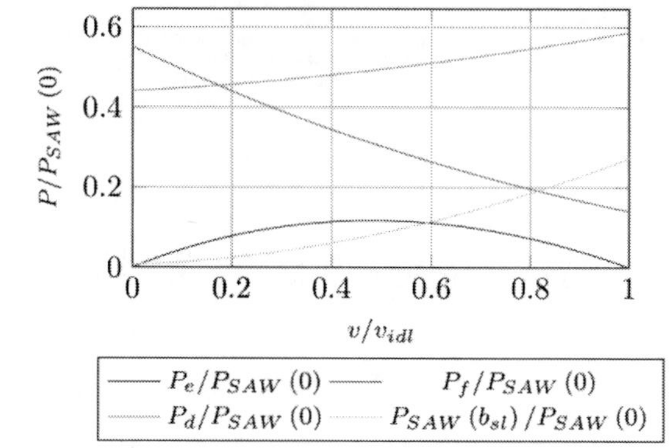


Fig. 8. Calculated effective power $P_e$, friction losses $P_f$, dynamic losses $P_d$ and remaining SAW power $P_{SAW}$ behind the slider for a SAW motor as described in [14]; Total contact force $F_N$ = 80 N; Assumed roughness $R_a$ = 1 nm due to used thin-film technology

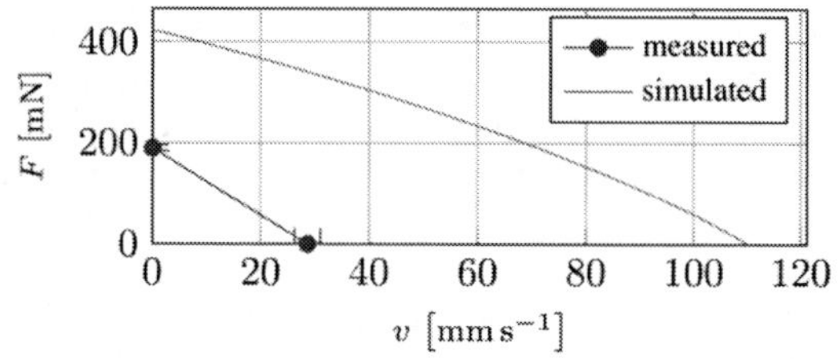


Fig. 9. Measured and simulated characteristic of SAW motor with non-piezoelectric stator material

The dynamic loss of one projection is the sum of normal and tangential dynamic power losses of all $j$ terms, corresponding to the *Fourier* polynominal. Fig. 8 shows the power components, calculated with this expanded motor model belonging to the SAW motor presented in [14]. It is obvious that dynamic losses cannot be neglected for high contact forces.

The comparison of measured motor parameters with calculated motor characteristics in Fig. 9 reveals a clear deviation between numerical model and manufactured motor. Analyzing the measured normal displacements on the manufactured stator, according to Fig. 10, suggests a moderate SAW quality. A high standing wave ratio close to the piezoelectric unit indicates parasitic bulk waves, emitted from the piezoelectric unit and reflected at the ground. Noticeable amplitude variation suggests inhomogenities of the stator. Roughness can be eliminated as an explanatory factor. However, the steel plate was heated and cooled down slowly to release material tensions and allow a high quality of flatness by lapping. This affects grain sizes in the scale of SAW wavelength and can cause the observed SAW quality issues [15]. Bulk waves can be reduced by a higher number of finger electrodes. Different manufacturing technologies or even other steel grades will decrease the grain size. We assume that both improvements will significantly reduce the gap between measurements and simulation.

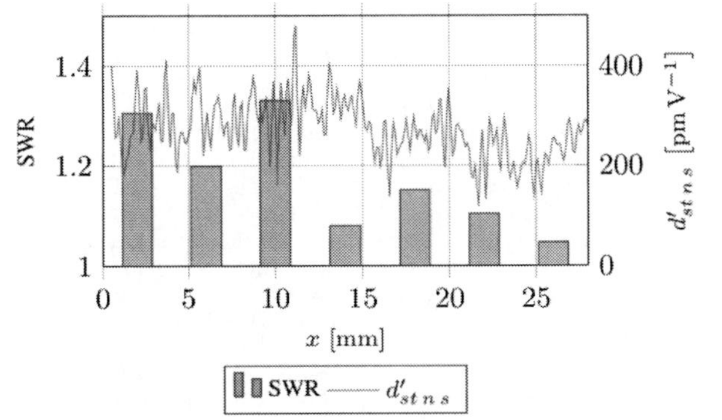


Fig. 10. Measured standing wave ratio (SWR) and relative amplitude $d'_{st,\,n\,s}$ of normal displacement of substrate surface along SAW traveling direction for SAW motor with non-piezoelectric stator material; SWR was sectionally determined by method of least squares

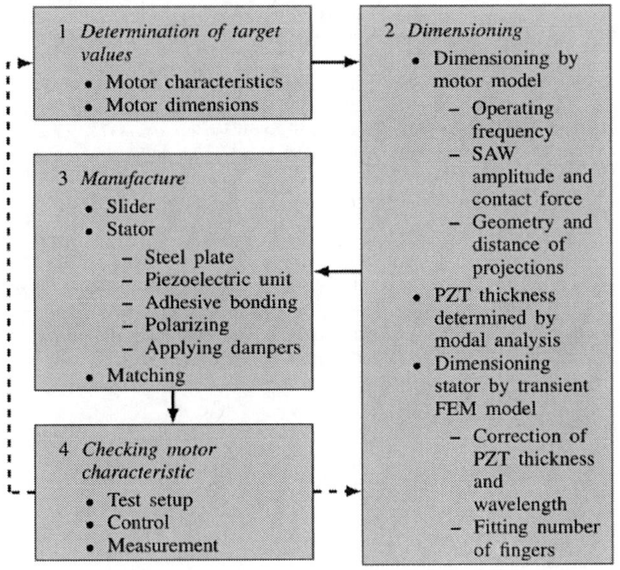


Fig. 11. Proposed procedure for designing SAW motors with steel stator

## III. Guidelines for Designing

This section presents the working steps to design and manufacture an SAW motor with non-piezoelectric stator material based on specified characteristics. These guidelines are the result of experiences we gathered by developing, manufacturing and testing the SAW motor. They are limited to motors with a PZT unit adhered on metallic substrate and a slider made from silicon. Refeeding of remaining SAW power is not considered. Our presented procedure is also visualized in Fig. 11.

1 *Determination of target values*
- Motor characteristics: Define blocking force and idling speed.
- Motor dimensions: The width of the motor is proportional to motor power by constant SAW amplitude. The length of the motor results from travel range and the dimensions of piezoelectric units and dampers.

2 *Dimensioning*
- Dimensioning by motor model:
  - Operating frequency: Higher operating frequencies result in higher idling speeds and lower blocking forces.
  - SAW amplitude and contact force: Here an optimization process is needed. The main target is to reach specified motor characteristic. The secondary target is to minimize the SAW amplitude for a higher efficiency.
  - Geometry and distance of projections: Projection diameters of about $20\,\mu m$ and projection spacings of about $40\,\mu m$ have been found as ideal structuring geometry in [16]. In addition, the efficiency of extraordinary motor characteristics can be optimized by varying that geometry.
- PZT thickness determined by modal analysis: Specify finger spacing by operating frequency and SAW speed. Vary thickness of PZT to reach targeted frequency for the first symmetric *Sezawa* mode.
- Dimensioning stator by transient FEM model:
  - Correction of PZT thickness and finger spacing: Vary parameters within an optimization to maximize the SAW displacement per voltage and the efficiency.
  - Fitting number of fingers: Vary this parameter to reach the relative SAW displacement, while respecting dielectric strength, tensile strengths and depolarization. As we observed a much higher relative SAW amplitude in simulation related to measurements, we recommend a safety of 30 for depolarization.

3 *Manufacture*
- Slider: Thin-layer technology is to be used without any special features.
- Stator:
  - Metal plate: Thickness must be more than triple wavelength. Lap and polish the stress-relieved plate. Roughen the bonding surface.
  - Piezoelectric unit: Saw out the PZT plate. Sputter a ground electrode on one side. Apply IDT by thick film technology on the other side. Both electrodes are made from gold.
  - Adhesive bonding: Ensure an electric contact between ground electrode and metal plate for later polarization. Furthermore, a mechanical wide-area contact with thin adhesive layer thickness is needed for a good transmission.
  - Polarizing: For normal polarization with $2\,MV\,m^{-1}$, conductive silver lacquer must be applied on the top surface and removed afterwards. Correct application and removing can be checked by resistance measurements.

   – Applying dampers: Apply viscoelastic material behind the piezoelectric units over a distance of ten wavelengths.
- Matching: Build up an impedance matching considering the measured stator impedance at operation frequency.

4 *Checking motor characteristic*
- Test setup: Connect stator with impedance matching, amplifier and waveform generator. Stator voltage can be checked directly by oscilloscope. Clean contact surfaces. Attach slider and magnets with iron counterplate carefully onto the stator.
- Control: Depending on input power drive the motor only in burst mode with sinusoidal excitation.
- Measurement: Measure idling speed by laser triangulation sensor and blocking force by force measuring device with force transducer crossing the travel path.

## IV. Conclusion

We have presented detailed guidelines for designing a novel type of SAW motor with non-piezoelectric stator material. Required numeric models are extensively described and discussed as well. With this, we enable manufacturing and further investigations into this motor type to improve its characteristics. We are optimistic that these improvements lead to compact linear motors with a high positioning accuracy, high power density and, moreover, an inexpensive manufacturing. The presented models and resulting verified guidelines should contribute to a market launch of SAW motors that will support the growing demand for compact linear actuators.

## Acknowledgment

The authors would like to thank Hagen Schmidt and Robert Weser of the Leibnitz Institute for Solid State and Materials Research in Dresden for the recurring friendly support with measurement equipment and professional advices. We also thank Sylvia Gebhardt and Susanne Tilke of the Fraunhofer Institute for Ceramic Technologies and Systems IKTS for the manufacture and mounting of piezoelectric units.

## References

[1] F. Zhang, W. Chen J. Lin, and Z. Wang, "Bidirectional linear ultrasonic motor using longitudinal vibrating transducers" IEEE Transactions on Ultrasonics, Ferroelectrics, and Frequency Control, IEEE, vol. 52.1, pp. 134–138, 2005. DOI: 10.1109/TUFFC.2005.1397358.

[2] K. Spanner, O. Vyshnevskyy, and W. Wischnewskiy, "New linear ultrasonic micromotor for precision mechatronic systems" Proceedings of the 10th International Conference on New Actuators (Actuator 2006), pp. 439–443, 2006.

[3] Y. Shi and C. Zhao, "A new standing-wave-type linear ultrasonic motor based on in-plane modes" Ultrasonics, Elsevier, vol. 51.4, pp. 397–404, 2011.

[4] Z. Wan and H. Hu, "Modeling and experimental analysis of the linear ultrasonic motor with in-plane bending and longitudinal mode", Ultrasonics, Elsevier, vol. 54.3, pp. 921–928, 2014. DOI: 10.1016/j.ultras.2013.11.004.

[5] M. Guo, S. Pan, J. Hu, C. Zhao, and S. Dong, "A small linear ultrasonic motor utilizing longitudinal and bending modes of a piezoelectric tube", IEEE Transactions on Ultrasonics, Ferroelectrics, and Frequency Control, IEEE, vol. 61.4, pp. 705–709, 2014. DOI: 10.1109/TUFFC.2014.2958.

[6] T. Shigematsu, M. K. Kurosawa, and K. Asai, "Nanometer stepping drives of surface acoustic wave motor", IEEE Transactions on Ultrasonics, Ferroelectrics, and Frequency Control, IEEE, vol. 50.4, pp. 376–385, 2003. DOI: 10.1109/TUFFC.2003.1197960.

[7] R. Günther, R. Richter, and J. Lienig, "Contributions to the development of an axisymmetric SAW motor with a stator made from non-piezoelectric material", Sensors and Actuators A: Physical, Elsevier, vol. 295, pp. 274–287, 2019. DOI: 10.1016/j.sna.2019.04.024.

[8] T. Shigematsu and M. K. Kurosawa, "Friction drive modeling of SAW motor using classical theory of contact mechanics", Proc. of 10th Conf. on New Actuators, pp. 444–448, 2006.

[9] I. A. Viktorov, "Rayleigh and Lamb Waves: Physical Theory and Applications: Translated from Russian", Plenum press, 1967.

[10] K. L. Johnson, "Normal contact of elastic solids – hertz theory", Contact Mechanics, Cambridge University Press, Ch. 4, pp. 84–106, 1985.

[11] J. L. Brown, "Sampling bandlimited periodic signals–an application of the DFT", IEEE Transactions on Education, IEEE, vol. 23.4, pp. 205–206, 1980. DOI: 10.1109/TE.1980.4321415.

[12] G. Merziger, G. Mühlbach, D. Wille, and T. Wirth, "Folgen, Reihen [Sequences, Series]", Formeln + Hilfen zur höheren Mathematik [Formulas + Helps for higher mathematics], Binomi, Edition 3, p. 76, 1999.

[13] G. M. L. Gladwell, "The calculation of mechanical impedances relating to an indenter vibrating on the surface of a semi-infinite elastic body", Journal of Sound and Vibration, vol. 8.2, pp. 215–228, 1968. DOI: 10.1016/0022-460X(68)90228-9.

[14] M. K. Kurosawa and T. Shigematsu, "Friction drive simulation of a SAW motor with slider surface texture variation", Advances in Science and Technology, Trans Tech Publ., vol. 54, pp. 366–371, 2008. DOI: 10.4028/www.scientific.net/AST.54.366.

[15] A. Fattah-Alhosseini and S. Vafaeian, "Comparison of electrochemical behavior between coarse-grained and fine-grained AISI 430 ferritic stainless steel by Mott-Schottky analysis and EIS measurements", Journal of Alloys and Compounds 639, pp. 301–307, 2015. DOI: 10.1016/j.jallcom.2015.03.142.

[16] M. K. Kurosawa, H. Itoh, K. Asai, M. Takasaki, and T. Higuchi, "Optimization of slider contact face geometry for surface acoustic wave motor", The 14th IEEE International Conference on MEMS, pp. 252–255, 2001. DOI: 10.1109/MEMSYS.2001.906526.

# Optical Flow Sensor Based on Thermal Time Constant Measurement

Jernej Hribar
Laboratory for Electro Optics and Sensory Systems
Faculty of Electrical Engineering and Computer Science
Maribor, Slovenia
e-mail: jernej.hribar@um.si

Prof. Dr. Denis Donlagic
Laboratory for Electro Optics and Sensory Systems
Faculty of Electrical Engineering and Computer Science
Maribor, Slovenia
denis.donlagic@um.si

*Abstract*— **This contribution presents a novel all-dielectric, all-optical microfluidic flow sensor based on thermal time constant measurement. The proposed sensor utilizes a single optical fiber positioned perpendicular to the flow in a glass capillary. A Vanadium-Doped Fiber was utilized, in combination with Fiber Bragg grating to measure the thermal time constant of the fiber. The fiber was heated periodically with a laser source. The temperature change of the fiber was observed, and the system's thermal time constant calculated simultaneously. The thermal time constant of the system correlates directly with the flow of the fluid. When the fiber was placed in a glass capillary with an inner diameter of 650 µm, flow rate measurement in the range from 0 ml/h to 300 ml/h was achievable. Furthermore, as shown in this contribution, the sensor was not sensitive to losses in the lead-in optical fiber or optical source power fluctuations, which is rarely the case with optical fiber sensors utilizing an optical fiber heater.**

***Keywords—optical fiber sensor; thermal time constant; flow measurement.***

## I. Introduction

Flow rate measurement is an essential procedure in a variety of applications. Ranging from the process, biomedical, microfluidic, petrochemical, and other industries, various principles have been employed; some have been tailored specifically for a given metering application. Conventional mechanical principles are well proven, and used in many industrial applications; however, they lack the potential for miniaturization. Therefore, a variety of thermal principles have been developed in the past which enable miniaturization. The majority of the anemometric or calorimetric sensors depend on electrical heating and sensing, which disables the application of such systems in electromagnetically polluted areas, at high temperatures and/or chemically aggressive environments. Many researchers have recently proposed using optical fiber setups for thermal flow metering, using various principles[1]–[12]. Cobalt or Vanadium-Doped Fibers (VDF) have been used [1]–[9][11][12] in calorimetric or anemometric setups because their use enables fast and controllable heating. Cobalt or vanadium doped fibers act as a heater. A standard pump diode is usually used as a photon supply for the Vanadium and Cobalt doped fibers, absorbing the light and transforming it to heat. However, anemometric and calorimetric principles are very sensitive to changes in the heating power delivered to the fiber, which is an issue that many optical fiber sensors cannot mitigate. Losses in connectors, fibers, and fluctuations of the source's optical output power are difficult to control, and usually demand complex and expensive compensation systems, making them non-competitive on the market. Matjasec and Donlagic[13] have shown that this issue can be avoided if the appropriate control technique is used in a thermal conductivity measurement setup. Instead of a constant power or constant temperature approach, a sinusoidally modulated heating source was employed, which overcame unavoidable fluctuations of heating power. Measurement of thermal time constant was used in their case to determine the thermal conductivity of the measured liquid. In this paper, this principle has been extended to measure flow rate. Measured thermal time constant is highly dependent on the flow velocity of the liquid surrounding the sensor, as is shown in the following sections.

One of the possible approaches that could mitigate the drawbacks mentioned above and simultaneously offer a reliable and straightforward design capable of flow measurement could be via the measurement of thermal time constant of a structure submerged in a flow. In this principle a time varying heat source is submerged in the fluids flow and thermal time constant is measured. Nusselt number (ratio of convective heat transfer and conductive heat transfer) increases with the increase of flow velocity around the sensor due to forced convection introduced with the flow. Such a system also enables implementation in a microfluidic environment if optical fiber technology is applied to measure the thermal constant. Simultaneously, optical fiber technology enables the use of the proposed measurement system in areas that present an unavoidable obstacle for classic electrical sensors, such as high temperatures, chemically harsh, or/and radiation polluted environments. Furthermore, simple construction and low-cost optical fibers enable the use of the proposed system in various applications, especially for lab-on-a-chip applications, where flow measurement is needed during the operation, and later the chip is discarded.

In this paper, we present an all silica, all-optical, all-dielectric, microfluidic flow sensor based on thermal time constant measurement. The proposed sensor cultivates principles from two sensors previously designed by our research group[10][13]. The proposed sensor is based on a single Vanadium-Doped Fiber with inscribed Fiber Bragg grating (FBG), which acts as a dynamic temperature sensor. FBG is a periodic change of the refractive index in the fiber core, which generates a wavelength specific dielectric mirror. With temperature increase of the FBG, the reflected wavelength increases accordingly. This setup enables measurement of the heat discharge from the heated surface, which correlates with the velocity of the fluid. The proposed sensor is highly insensitive to the variations or the changes of the heating power, which is rarely the case with other flow sensors based on thermal principles. Moreover, due to its all-silica design, it possesses all the advantages of optical fiber sensors, for example, application in electromagnetically polluted areas, in high temperatures or chemically harsh environments. The remainder of the paper is organised as follows. Section 2 presents sensor's design; Section 3 presents the manufacturing method and experimental setup for the measurements. Section 4 presents the Results. Conclusions are made in the last, Section 5.

## II. SENSOR DESIGN

The presented sensor is a redesign from the previous work of Matjasec and Donlagic[13]. Their sensor is redesigned to employ FBG instead of the Fabry-Perot sensing cavity. Redesign allows the sensor to be shorter and inserted in a capillary with an inner diameter of 650 µm. It also enables the use of commercially available high-speed FBG interrogators.

The addition of small amounts of Vanadium to the core of silica optical fibers has been found to increase absorption of light with wavelengths lower than 1000 nm [14][15]. The VDF was initially drawn to 125 µm diameter with a core diameter of about 9 µm. A Medium Power Laser Diode(MPLD) was used, with a central wavelength of 980 nm. Such diodes are usually used as pumping sources for Erbium fiber amplifiers. MPLD is modulated sinusoidally, which causes the VDF to heat up and cool down in the fluid flow. To decrease the natural time constant of the system, the sensing fiber was etched to a diameter of 35 µm. This also decreases the drag in the channel, which correlates with

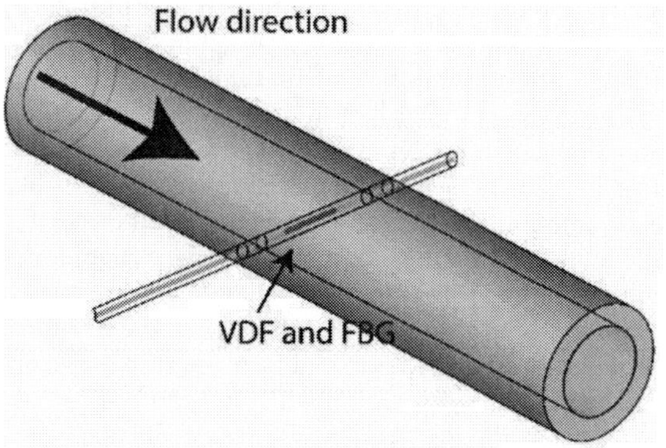


Figure 1. Schematic view of the proposed sensor

fluid velocity. The sensing fiber was positioned perpendicularly to the flow direction, in the middle of the flow channel. The sensor assembly is shown in Fig. 1, and the manufactured sensor is shown in Fig. 2.

The heating segment was a 250 µm long piece positioned in the middle of the flow channel. It was spliced to an HI 1060 fiber which served as the lead-in fiber. The Vanadium-Doped Fiber was custom made and is described in [16]. The fiber used in this work can be found as fiber 3 in Table 2 of [16]. The fiber's initial diameter was 125 µm with a core diameter of 9 µm, which was later etched as described further below. The Fiber Bragg Grating was inscribed in the section of the VDF which enabled thermal time constant measurement. The proposed sensor was positioned in a glass capillary with an inner diameter of 650 µm and an outer diameter of 1000 µm.

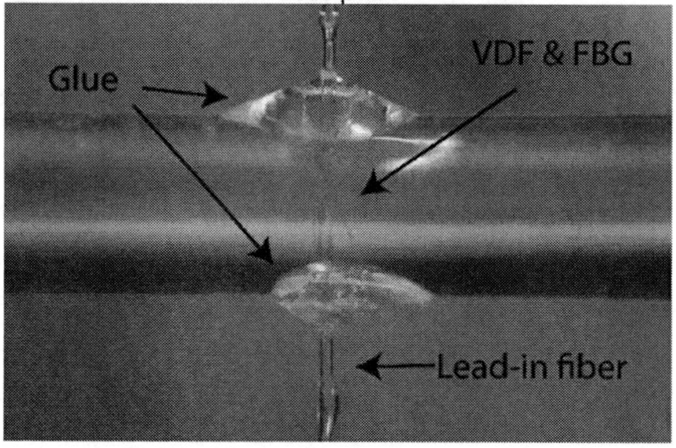


Figure 2. Photograph of the manufactured sensor

## III. MANUFACTURING PROCEDURE AND EXPERIMETNAL SETUP

The manufacturing process of the sensing fiber consisted of a simple cleave and splice sequence. As shown in Fig. 3a, a cleaved piece of VDF was spliced to the lead-in single mode HI-1060 fiber. This was accomplished in a standard arc fusion splicer. The VDF was then cleaved at the length of 250 µm from the splice, under an optical microscope to ensure the correct length of the VDF. The remaining fiber was spliced to the lead-out coreless fiber, as seen in Fig. 3b, which was cleaved at a length about 1 mm away from the VDF. The FBG was inscribed using a femtosecond laser and positioning system as shown in Fig. 3c. The desired length, reflectivity, and Bragg wavelength of the FBG can be selected with such a system. With a desired length of 250 µm, we achieved reflectivity of about 10% at Bragg wavelength 1543 nm. The sensing fiber was then etched in a 40% HF solution for about 50 minutes to decrease its diameter from 125 µm to about 35 µm, as shown in Fig. 3d. Fiber diameter reduction shortens the thermal response time and, consequently, enables the use of higher modulation frequencies. The same femtosecond laser system was used to drill holes with diameter of about 45 µm in the glass capillary, which served as a flow channel (Fig. 3e). Drilled holes were oversized to enable easier insertion of the etched fiber. High laser power was used to ablate the material. Lastly, the fiber was inserted into the capillary by hand, under an optical microscope. To determine the axial position of the FBG in the fiber, a red laser pointer was coupled in the fiber produced by the above-mentioned method, and the position of the FBG was clearly visible with the eye due to diffraction of the red light on imperfections caused by the manufacturing method. This supported flawless positioning of the sensing fiber in the middle of the flow channel. High viscosity 2-component epoxy glue was used to seal off the holes in the capillary. A fully assembled sensor is depicted in Fig. 2 under an optical microscope.

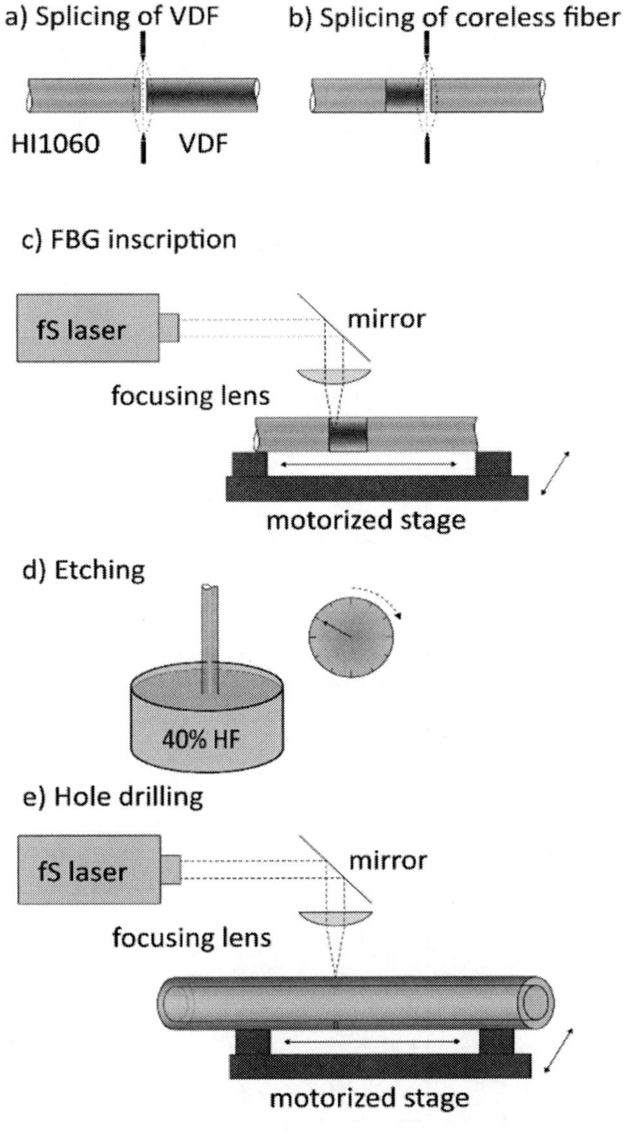


Figure 3. Manufacturing procedure

Two interconnected subsystems were used for thermal time constant measurement: A heating power delivery subsystem and dynamic temperature measurement and processing subsystem. Both subsystems are depicted in Fig. 4. The heating power delivery subsystem consisted of a medium power laser diode (MPLD) with central wavelength of 980 nm, which was connected to an appropriate driver. The driver was controlled with a programmable sine function generator. The programmable sine generator enabled control over the frequency and amplitude of the modulation. The dynamic temperature measurement subsystem consisted of a high speed FBG interrogator (FAZ I4E). The Bragg wavelength data were transferred in real time to a PC using LabVIEW. The sensing fiber was connected to both subsystems with a Wavelength Division Multiplexer (WDM), which enables coupling of the light from the MPLD and FBG interrogator.

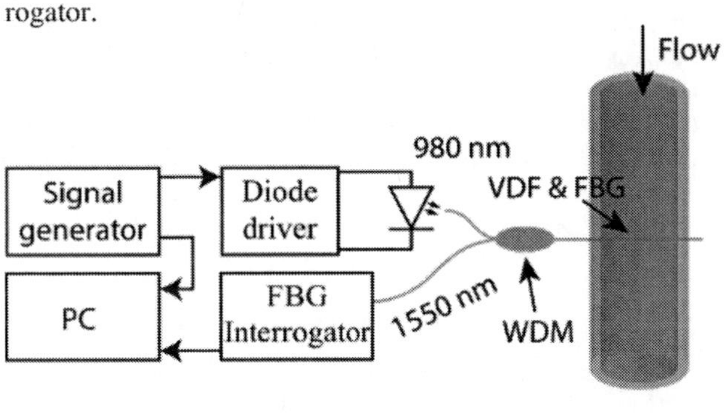


Figure 4. Interrogation setup

## IV. SENSOR OPERATION AND THEROY

Two principles could be used to measure flow rate with the presented setup: a) Measurement of the total/accumulative change of the heated object's temperature due to the application of the known heating power, and b) Measurement of the thermal time constant of the heated object. While the first approach offers more simple interrogation software, it requires that the delivered heating power is known and constant. This is a drawback of many optical fiber sensors, because losses in the optical systems are unpredictable and are hard to evaluate. Therefore, we decided to employ the second technique, where the thermal time constant of the heated fiber is measured. The MPLD was driven by a current that was modulated with a raised sine function, which resulted in further raised-sine modulation of the output optical power. This sine-modulated optical power was then delivered to the optical sensor inserted in the fluid flow. The VDF absorbed the optical power, which resulted in a sinusoidal time-dependent variolation of the VDF's temperature. This time-dependent temperature variation was then determined with the use of FBG and a high-speed interrogator. Bragg wavelength variation followed MPLD sine modulation but was delayed/lagged in time to the modulation signal. A lag/phase difference $\Delta\varphi$ between the MPLD sine modulation and FBG's wavelength (temperature) change was correlated to the heated fiber's thermal time constant $\tau$ as:

$$\tau = -tg(\Delta\varphi) / 2\pi f \; ; \; -\pi < \Delta\varphi < \pi \qquad (1)$$

Where $f$ represents the frequency of the MPLD modulation and $\Delta\varphi$ representes the measured phase delay between the modulation and temperature signal. The fiber's (sensor's) thermal time constant $\tau$ and the thermal conductivity $k_f$ are related through the following expression [16]:

$$\tau = p_s \, c_s \, b^2 / k_f \, Nu \qquad (2)$$

where $p_s$ represents silica specific density, $c_s$ silica specific heat, b fiber radius and Nu the Nusselt number. Silica specific density, silica specific heat and fiber radius were, in our case, constant. The Nusselt number, however, is a fluido-dynamic parameter, which represents the ratio between convective to conductive heat transfer at a boundary in a fluid. We can conclude that, when the flow rate around the sensor increases, the Nusselt number increases accordingly, due to forced convection, consequently changing the thermal time constant.

## V. Measurement Results

The proposed and experimentally produced sensor was configured and tested in a liquid flow control system. We used a calibrated syringe pump, which provided the possibility to set abslotue flow rates over a broad range of flow rate values. Connections between the syringe, sensor and waste beaker were made with silicone tubing with an inner diameter of 1mm. In the first set of experiments the sensor`s response for flow ranging from 0 to 300 ml/h is shown. Isopropyl alcohol was used for all experiments. The heating peak-to-peak power amplitude corresponded to 34 mW, and the frequency was set to 20 Hz. This frequency was selected because the sensor`s natural time constant (no-flow condition) corresponded to around 5 ms. To establish a continuous flow rate measurement through the sensor, the phase difference between the FBG's temperature signals and modulation signal was measured continuously over time. This was accomplished by performing a Fast Fourier Transformation (FFT) continuously on the FBG temperature versus time and heating power versus time signals acquired within 1 s long time intervals. The phase difference between both signals was then obtained by subtracting the phases of the components in the FFT that correspond to the excitation frequency. This provided a robust and noise-tolerant calculation of the phase difference between both signals. The phase difference between both signals was converted to a time constant, using Eq.1. An example of measured time constant versus flow rate, using IPA and the above-mentioned excitation parameters, is shown in Fig. 5. for the flow rate between 0 and 300 ml/h.

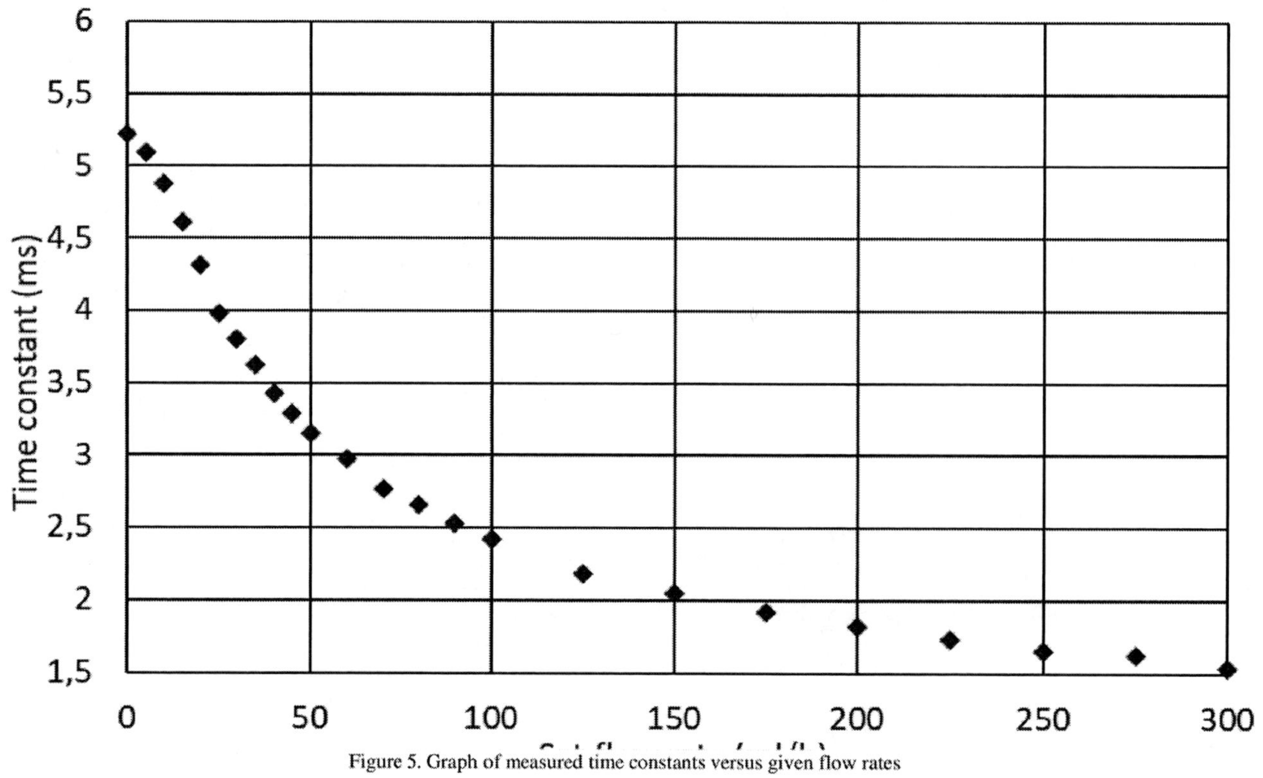


Figure 5. Graph of measured time constants versus given flow rates

As seen in Fig. 5, the flow rate and measured thermal time constant are proportionally inverse, as predicted by Equation 2.

Most thermo-optic fiber-based flow sensors reported in the literature [1][4][5][12][17] assume that the delivered heating optical power is known and constant. Deviation from this assumption usually translates directly into the increased measurement uncertainty. The proposed sensor is, however, due to the application of the thermal time constant measurment principle, highly tolerant to the variations in delivered heating power, as demonstrated by Fig. 6. Figure 6 shows the experiment where the flow rate was measured at three substantially different amplitudes of sinusoidal modulation optical power. The results in Fig. 6 demonstrate that there is no correlation between total delivered optical power to the Vanadium-Doped Fiber and the measured thermal time constant. However, it should also be stressed that, at lower flow velocities, the delivered power shall be limited to prevent reaching the fluid's boiling point, as this disturbs the flow and affects measurement. On the other hand, very low optical powers lead to the degradation of signal amplitude, and, thus, to reduced signal to noise ratio, which is reflected further in degradation of the measurement resolution.

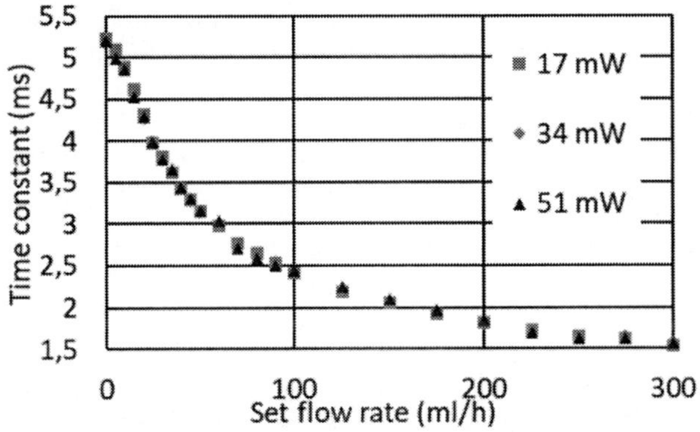


Figure 6. Dependency of measured result from heating power

The last set of performed experiments was devoted to experimental investigation of the proposed sensor's measurement resolution. The sensor`s resolution was demonstrated at different flows using a siphoning effect to enable a pulsation free and stable fluid flow. Known and predetermined amounts of liquid were added to the upper beaker at approximately 20 s intervals. The flow rate was verified using a scale by weighting the change of mass of the liquid in time. An example of the sensor`s resolution demonstration is, thus, presented in Figs. 7 and 8 at initial flow rates of around 25 ml/h and 210 ml/h, respectively.

By comparing the sensor's output change with the measurement of noise levels in Figs. 7 and 8 we concluded that the sensor`s resolution was about 0.81 ml/h for flow rates around 25 ml/h, and 3.1 ml/h for flow rates around 200 ml/h. Altogether, we can conclude that the proposed sensor's overall resolution was 3.1ml/h for the flow range from 0 to 300 ml/h, which corresponded to about 1.03% of the full scale resolution.

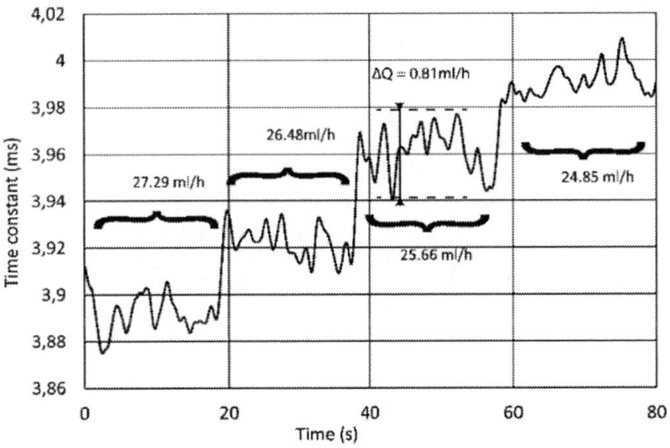


Figure 7. Demonstration of sensor resolution and time response at low flow rates

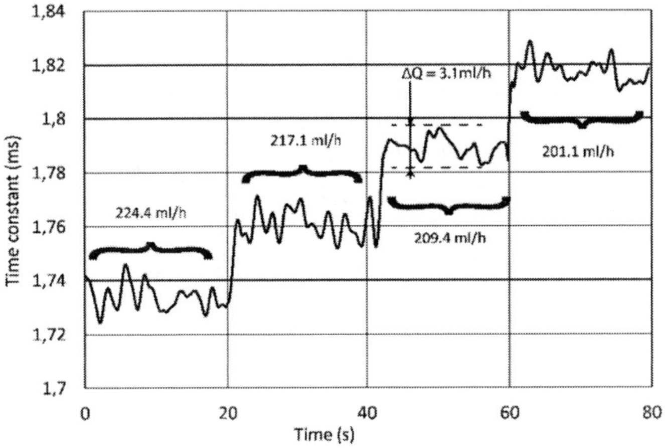


Figure 8. Demonstration of sensor resolution and time response at low flow rates

## VI. CONCLUSIONS

An all-fiber, all-silica microfluidic flow sensor based on thermal time constant measurement was presented in this paper. The sensor was based on a short section of Vanadium-Doped Fiber with inscribed Fiber Bragg Grating. The sensor was heated optically and periodically in time by a laser diode, while the temperature change was observed, and the phase difference calculated between the modulated and measured temperature signal. This phase difference was used to calculate the thermal time constant of the sensor, which, in accord with the presented theoretical background, decreased when the flow of the fluid was introduced around the sensor. The sensor was packaged in a glass capillary with an inner diameter of 650 μm, and tested for different flow rates using IPA. The proposed sensor was simple to construct and interrogate. It offers two distinct advantages over other optical fiber flow sensors. Firstly, it's very simple, single fiber design offers the possibility in microfluidic applications where space is limited. Secondly, its immunity to varying losses in optical fibers offers the possibility to use it in rugged areas with minimal maintenance and human interference during its lifetime. The experimental version of the sensor was demonstrated for flow rate measurement from 0 to 300 ml/h with a full-scale resolution of around 1%. All the experiments were conducted with IPA, and calibration of the sensor would be needed in a commercial application for the given fluid. However, with measurement of the time constant of the liquid when there is no flow presented in the channel, an in-situ calibration is possible. The sensor is sensitive to debris presented in the liquid, especially microfibers, which clog the flow channel and interfere with the time constant measurement. Moreover, any two-phase flow (gas and liquid) would also interfere with the measurement and render it unreliable. The proposed sensor also possesses all the advantages associated with fiber-optic sensors, such as, for example, dielectric and chemically inert design, electrical passivity, immunity to electromagnetic interference, small size, and biocompatibility. The proposed sensor can measure the flow velocities of aggressive fluids and enables use of long lead-in fibers to measure flow in remote locations separated from the optoelectronic interrogation unit. Moreover, the authors believe that the sensor's upscaling and downscaling without degradation of properties is possible. While other flow measurement solutions might offer better dynamic range and resolution, the proposed sensors' simple and low-cost design enables use in single-use lab-on-a-chip applications and biomedical applications.

## ACKNOWLEDGMENT

This work was supported by Slovenian Research Agency Grants J2-8192 and P2-0368.

## REFERENCES

1. Z. Liu, M.-L. V. Tse, A. P. Zhang, and H.-Y. Tam, "Integrated microfluidic flowmeter based on a micro-FBG inscribed in Co^2+-doped optical fiber," Opt. Lett. **39**(20), (2014).
2. J. Ma, G. Wang, L. Jin, K. Oh, and B.-O. Guan, "Photothermally generated bubble on fiber (BoF) for precise sensing and control of liquid flow along a microfluidic channel," Opt. Express **27**(14), (2019).
3. G. Liu, Q. Sheng, W. Hou, and M. Han, "Optical fiber vector flow sensor based on a silicon Fabry–Perot interferometer array," Opt. Lett. **41**(20), 4629 (2016).
4. B. Zhou, H. Jiang, C. Lu, and S. He, "Hot Cavity Optical Fiber Fabry-Perot Interferometer as a Flow Sensor with Temperature Self-calibrated," J. Light. Technol. **PP**(99), (2016).
5. R. Chen, A. Yan, Q. Wang, and K. P. Chen, "Fiber-optic flow sensors for high-temperature environment operation up to 800°C," Opt. Lett. **39**(13), (2014).
6. L. H. Cho, C. Lu, A. P. Zhang, and H. Y. Tam, "Fiber Bragg grating anemometer with reduced pump power-dependency," IEEE Photonics Technol. Lett. **25**(24), (2013).
7. R. qing Lv, H. kun Zheng, Y. Zhao, and Y. fei Gu, "An optical fiber sensor for simultaneous measurement of flow rate and temperature in the pipeline," Opt. Fiber Technol. **45**, (2018).
8. V. Lien and F. Vollmer, "Microfluidic flow rate detection based on integrated optical fiber cantilever," Lab Chip **7**(10), (2007).
9. Z. Chen, Z. Guo, X. Mu, Q. Li, X. Wu, and H. Y. Fu, "Packaged microbubble resonator optofluidic flow rate sensor based on Bernoulli Effect," Opt. Express **27**(25), 36932 (2019).
10. J. Hribar and D. Donlagic, "Optical flow sensor based on the thermal time-of-flight measurement," Opt. Express **29**(6), 8846 (2021).
11. J. Hribar and D. Donlagic, "Fiber-Optic Boiling Point Sensor for Characterization of Liquids," IEEE Sens. J. **20**(14), (2020).
12. Y. Li, G. Yan, L. Zhang, and S. He, "Microfluidic flowmeter based on micro "hot-wire" sandwiched Fabry-Perot interferometer," Opt. Express **23**(7), (2015).
13. Z. Matjasec and D. Donlagic, "All-optical, all-fiber, thermal conductivity sensor for identification and characterization of fluids," Sensors Actuators, B Chem. **242**, (2017).
14. M. K. Davis and M. J. F. Digonnet, "Measurements of thermal effects in fibers doped with cobalt and vanadium," J. Light. Technol. **18**(2), (2000).
15. P. C. Schultz, "Optical Absorption of the Transition Elements in Vitreous Silica," J. Am. Ceram. Soc. **57**(7), (1974).
16. Z. Matjasec, S. Campelj, and D. Donlagic, "All-optical, thermo-optical path length modulation based on the vanadium-doped fibers," Opt. Express **21**(10), (2013).
17. J. Cheng, W. Zhu, Z. Huang, and P. Hu, "Experimental and simulation study on thermal gas flowmeter based on fiber Bragg grating coated with silver film," Sensors Actuators, A Phys. **228**, (2015).

# Analysis of Adhesive Layer Material Influence on Transmission Characteristics of Plasmonic Based Biosensor with Nano-Hole Array

Ilya Belyakov, Nicholas Pfeifle, Merhdad Irannejad, Kingsley Wong, Emma Belliveau and Mustafa Yavuz,
Waterloo Institute for Nanotechnology
University of Waterloo
Waterloo, ON, Canada
e-mail: belyakov.bmstu@gmail.com

***Abstract*— Noble metal thin films have good optical properties as is required for Surface Plasmon Resonance (SPR) biosensors. The use of such films is often limited by their poor adhesion to glass substrates. It makes them susceptible to critical mechanical damage, creating a barrier for use outside laboratory. An intermediate adhesive layer can solve this problem but will affect the biosensor's optical properties.**

***Keywords-Surface Plasmon Resonance; NHA; EOT.***

## I. Introduction

Thin films of noble metals are well known for their good optical properties for biosensors. Among these noble thin films, gold films are suffered from poor adhesion to the oxide glass substrates. An intermediate adhesive layer can solve this problem such as Titanium and Tantalum, but it will affect the gold thin film biosensor optical performance. Among different type of sacrificial layer Aluminum (Al), Titanium (Ti), Tantalum (Ta), Chromium (Cr), and Tungsten (W) are the most promising candidates for gold based Extraordinary Optical Transmission (EOT) applications [1] [2].

## II. Numerical Simulations

The Surface Plasmon Resonance (SPR) sensor is based on the interaction between light and metal nanoparticles. A number of numerical methods are used to solve Maxwell's equations; however, a Finite Difference Time Domain (FDTD) method has been widely applied to study the interaction of an electromagnetic wave and surrounding medium and objects. In this study, a plane wave of linearly polarized light along the Y-axis ($\lambda$center = 575 nm with $\lambda$span = 350 nm) which propagates along the Z-axis, was used. The background environment was taken as water with a refractive index n=1.333. A periodic Nanohole Structure (NHA) with hole radius of 100nm, gold film thickness of 100 nm was considered in this study. The effect of five different metals were considered as an adhesive film with different thicknesses in the range of 2 nm to 25nm on optical performance of a NHA array as a biosensor. The calculation cell was considered as 400×400×1500 nm3, and the Periodic Boundary Condition (PBC) was used in the X- and Y-directions. Whilst the Anisotropic Perfect Matching Layer (APML) was used in the Z-direction as an absorbing boundary condition. The calculation grid resolution was as high as 1 to 3 nm in the calculation time was set as 200 fs. The transmission spectra were calculated using an X-Y monitor at 150 nm away from the gold NHA surface.

## III. Results and Conclusion

After a series of numerical analysis by targeting different sacrificial layers and thicknesses, it was found that using chromium film has no effect on the transmission properties of the NHA structure, while using tungsten as a sacrificial layer resulted in 12% and 19% increases in the transmission intensity of the resonance peaks at the wavelengths of 624 nm and 762 nm, respectively. It was also found that by using tantalum and titanium sacrificial films an extra resonance pea was recorded at the wavelength of 720 nm with transmission of 18% which could be attributed to the surface plasmon resonance of the sacrificial layer. The sacrificial layer resonance wavelength of the NHA structure with titanium intermediate layer was recorded at the wavelength of 740 nm with transmission intensity of 27.5%.

In conclusion, aluminum is a promising candidate as a sacrificial layer for NHA biosensors to achieve higher sensitivity and Figure of Merit (FOM). More analysis on the effects of using aluminum as an intermediate layer is underway and its results will be presented in due course.

## References

[1] X. Fan et al., "Assembly of gold nanoparticles into aluminum nanobowl array", Scientific Reports, vol. 7, no. 1, 2017. Available: 10.1038/s41598-017-02552-z.

[2] J. Bhattarai, M. Maruf and K. Stine, "Plasmonic-Active Nanostructured Thin Films", Processes, vol. 8, no. 1, p. 115, 2020. Available: 10.3390/pr8010115.

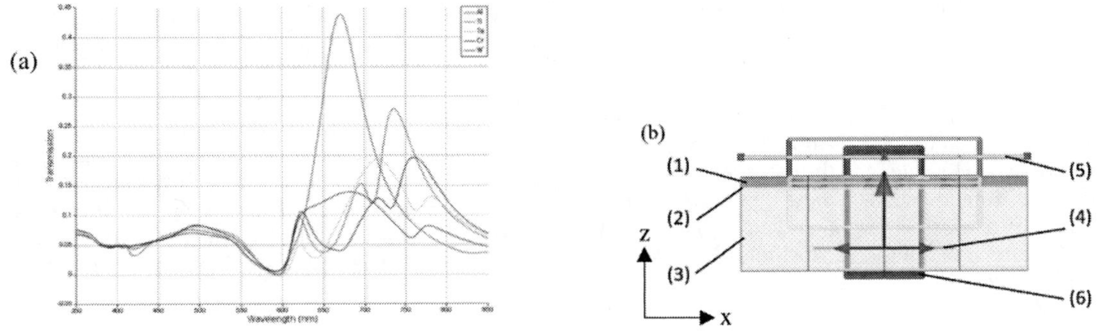


Figure 1. (a) Recorded transmission spectrum for various adhesive layer materials with the same geometrical properties. (b) Lumerical FDTD simulation, (1) NHA structure, (2) sacrificial layer (3) substrate, (4) light source, (5) T_monitor, (6) FDTD region

# Study on Effective Coverage of Low-Cost LoRa Devices

Laura García, Sandra Sendra, Jose M. Jimenez, Jaime Lloret
Integrated Management Coastal Research Institute
Universitat Politècnica de València
Valencia, Spain
e-mail: laugarg2@teleco.upv.es, sansenco@upv.es, jojiher@dcom.upv.es, jlloret@dcom.upv.es

Pascal Lorenz
Network and Telecommunication Research Group
University of Haute Alsace
Colmar, France
e-mail: lorenz@ieee.org

*Abstract*—**The use of LoRa has extended to varied applications, such as precision agriculture, oceanography, or Smart Cities. The advertised long-range coverage is one of the main claims of this wireless technology. However, the effective coverage of the more affordable Long-Range (LoRa) devices may not provide the connectivity that is expected. Therefore, it is necessary to know the effective coverage of the LoRa devices available in the market in order to design a LoRa network. In this paper, a coverage test of LoRa with low-cost electronic devices is performed. The tests measured the Received Signal Strength Indicator (RSSI) and were performed with the 433 MHz and 868 MHz frequency bands, antennas with gains of 3 dBi and 5dBi, and all the Spreading Factor (SF) configurations. The results show that bad signal quality is received at distances of 1 km approximately and thus, the use of low-cost devices for larger distances is not advised.**

***Keywords- LoRa; Coverage; RSSI; Spreading Factor; Gain.***

## I. INTRODUCTION

The introduction of wireless communications in varied scenarios, such as agriculture, oceanography, and the rise of Smart City solutions have led to the development of long-range wireless technologies, such as LoRa. LoRa is the specification of the physical layer and determines the modulation of this technology. One of the key aspects of the LoRa modulation is the Spreading Factor (SF), which indicates that the signal encompasses a bigger range of frequencies [1]. The main LoRa frequencies are 433 MHz, 868 MHz, and 915 MHz, which should be utilized according to the regulations of the location where the LoRa devices are deployed. On the other hand, the Medium Access Control (MAC) is specified by the Low Power Wide Area Network (LoRaWAN) protocol [2]. The nodes communicate with the gateway by forming a star topology. There can be multiple gateways to receive the data. Furthermore, three different device classes with variations in the amount of idle and on time are contemplated. However, as different technological solutions have different needs, new protocols and architectures for LoRa wireless communications have been designed [3]. These type of solutions substitutes LoRaWAN with the proposed protocols.

The use of LoRa has been contemplated for the detection of forest fires with systems that display the current data forwarded by the deployed nodes through a webpage [4]. The use of LoRa networks with multiple hops for Precision Agriculture (PA) is contemplated as well [3]. Monitoring infrastructures, such as a medieval aqueduct is also possible with multi-hop LoRa networks [5]. Furthermore, deploying LoRa sensing buoys [6] allows monitoring the state of the seas and transmitting the data to devices located at far distances, such as on-land stations. In order to design a deployment strategy for the aforementioned scenarios, aspects, such as coverage or energy consumption must be considered. However, the advertised transmission distances and energy consumption may not be the effective values reached by LoRa devices.

The official site of The Things Network advertises record LoRaWAN distances of 832 km [7]. Although this distance is obtained for specific LoRa settings, the advertised LoRa maximum distance is up to 15 km in line-of-sight deployments and up to 5 km in urban environments [1]. A few studies have been performed to determine the coverage of LoRa devices in different environments, such as urban areas with varied densities [8-10]. Some of them obtained results of 10 km for line-of-sight [9] or 8 km with a high Packet Loss Ratio [10]. However, these studies either do not specify the height of the transmitter and receiver nodes, or the node is located at the top of a building. Therefore, more coverage tests with other deployment configurations should be studied.

Another advertised aspect is its low cost. There are plenty of available devices in the low-cost price range. Furthermore, these devices are often coupled with low-cost antennas with low gains. Therefore, cost-effective solutions may obtain less coverage when utilizing LoRa. However, there are no studies available where low-cost devices are tested to determine the coverage that can be achieved with the use of this type of node. In this paper, the coverage of LoRa low-cost nodes considering different frequency bands, SF, and antennas. The Received Signal Strength Indicator (RSSI) was measured at different distances for each of the configurations. The tests were performed in a line-of-sight deployment where the transmitter was static, and the receiver moved to different measuring points.

The rest of the paper is organized as follows. Section 2 presents the related work. The description of the testbed is performed in Section 3. The results are discussed in Section 4. Lastly, the conclusion and future work are commented in Section 5.

## II. RELATED WORK

Although more coverage studies of LoRa devices are necessary, there are some studies that have evaluated the performance of LoRa communications. Fabrizio J. Grión et al. performed in [8] a coverage study of LoRa networks in urban environments. Firstly, coverage tests were performed in cities with different densities of buildings so as to develop a model to determine the coverage of a certain area through simulations. The utilized frequency was 915 MHz with a gain of 6 dBi for the transmission antenna and 0 dBi for the reception antenna. Results show a good similarity between the tests perform in the city and the simulations. Madoune R. Seye et al. evaluated the coverage of LoRa performing tests utilizing the 868 MHz frequency band, a spreading factor of 12, and a transmission power of 14 dBm [10]. The emitter was placed at the top of a building and the receiver moved to different zones in an 8 km radius. Furthermore, the results show a packet loss ratio of 13% for distances between 0 and 2 km and up to 70% for distances between 6 and 8 km. Madoune R. Seye et al. also performed coverage tests in the Dakar peninsula to develop a path loss model for LoRa [11]. The tests were performed for the 868 MHz frequency band and a transmit power of 14 dBm. The results showed that the Dakar peninsula could be entirely on the area of coverage with a maximum acceptable RSSI of -120 dBm, which leads to a 40% Packet Error Rate. Moreover, if the maximum admissible RSSI is reduced to -110 dBm, the Packet Error Rate (PER) is reduced to 20% but the connectivity is not provided to the entire peninsula. Lastly, Jansen C. Liando et al. conducted varied tests to determine the performance of LoRa [9]. The results showed that LoRa was able to achieve a coverage of 10 km in line-of-sight deployments but is greatly affected by obstacles. Furthermore, the authors state that the reduced energy consumption is only achieved with certain parameter configurations. Lastly, the gateway was able to provide support to 6000 nodes with less than 70% of Packet Reception Ratio (PRR).

LoRa has been compared with other wireless technologies as well. Mads Lauridsen et al. compared the coverage provided by different wireless technologies, such as LoRa, SigFox, General Packet Radio Service (GPRS), and NarrowBand-Internet of Things (NB-IoT) [12] through simulation experiments. The results show the best coverage results and Maximum Coupling Loss performance for NB-IoT. However, LoRa and SigFox obtained link loss results with an average of 3dB lower values than that of NB-IoT. Lastly, outage probabilities lower than 5% were obtained for NB-IoT and SigFox. Benny Vejlgaard et al. performed a comparison between GPRS, SigFoz, LoRa, and NB-IoT in an area of 8000 km2 [13]. Both indoor and outdoor deployments were considered. For outdoor tests, all technologies obtained more than 99% of coverage. Furthermore, the results showed that NB-IoT was the only wireless technology that provided connectivity in indoor settings with a failure rate below 5%. SigFox obtained a failure rate of 12%, while LoRa and GPRS were not apt for indoor transmissions.

The interference LoRa devices cause to each other in multi-hop network deployments was evaluated by Guibing Zhu et al. [14]. Both simulations and experiments with LoRa transceivers were performed. The results showed that the higher the SF, the higher the immunity to collisions for both transmissions with the same SF and transmissions with different SF. Furthermore, the authors proposed the use of SF-pipeline and concurrent transmission in multi-hop LoRa networks to allow faster packet transmissions.

Lastly, other uses for LoRa include deploying the devices on drones or floating structures. Mario Marchese et al. presented a proposal for a LoRa Gateway on an Unmanned Aerial Vehicle (UAV) [15]. Different scenarios were considered, such as transmitting to a satellite through a UAV gateway and deploying the gateway on the base station. The 868 MHz frequency band was considered, and Arduino nodes and a Raspberry Pi gateway were the selected electronic devices. Laboratory tests were performed to determine the RSSI for different densities. Furthermore, Liu Xia et al. presented in [6] the Oriented omnidirectional perceptual coverage algorithm (VFOPCA) to increase the coverage of LoRa sensor buoys. Simulations tests were performed to compare the performance of the proposed algorithm to the virtual force algorithm. The results showed a better performance of the proposed algorithm with lower energy consumption and higher convergence speed.

Albeit there are some LoRa coverage tests, the available studies do not compare the results for different SF values, do not indicate the utilized devices, or use a very high placement of the emitter antenna. Therefore, there is a need for more studies to expand the knowledge on the effective coverage of LoRa devices. In this paper, we address this need by studying the signal quality of LoRa low-cost devices with different low-cost antennas.

## III. TESTBED DESCRIPTION

In this section, the description of the utilized devices and performed tests is provided.

The utilized devices were Heltec LoRa/WiFi 32 nodes [16] for both emitter and receiver (see Figure 1). These nodes include an Organic Light-Emitting Diode (OLED) display and 36 pins. 433 MHz and 868 MHz nodes were used to perform tests with both frequency bands. The characteristics of the node are presented in Table 1.

Three different types of antennas were utilized. Two antennas for the 433 MHz frequency band were tested. The first antenna has a 3dBi gain and a Voltage Standing Wave Ratio (VSWR) below or equal to 1.5 (see Figure 2). Its working temperature range remains between -40 ºC and 85 ºC. Lastly, it has an input impedance of 50 Ω and a maximum input power of 10 W.

TABLE I. CHARACTERISTICS OF THE NODES.

| | |
|---|---|
| ***Tx Power*** | 17 dB |
| ***Frequency*** | 433 MHz and 868 MHz |
| ***SF*** | 7,8,9,10,11,12 |
| ***Signal Bandwidth*** | 125 KHz |
| ***Coding rate*** | 4/5 |
| ***Preamble length*** | 8 Symbols |
| ***Height of the antenna*** | 1.57 m |

Figure 1. Utilized Heltec devices.

Figure 2. 433 MHz antenna with a gain of 3dBi.

The second 433 MHz antenna has a gain of 5 dBi (see Figure 3). It has a Sub-Miniature A (SMA) connector, a VSWR ≤ 1.5, an input impedance of 50 Ω, maximum power of 50 W, and a working temperature range between -40 °C and 60°C.

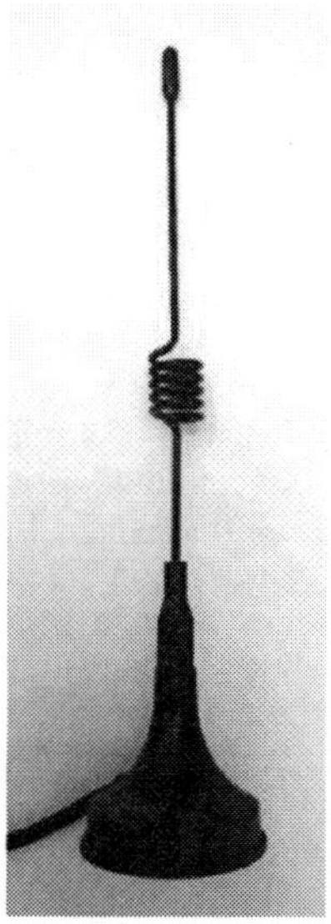

Figure 3. 433 MHz antenna with a gain of 5dBi.

Lastly, the antenna for the tests performed with the 868 MHz frequency band is presented in Figure 4. It has a gain of 3 dBi, a VSWR ≤ 1.5, maximum power of 10 W, and an input impedance of 50 Ω.

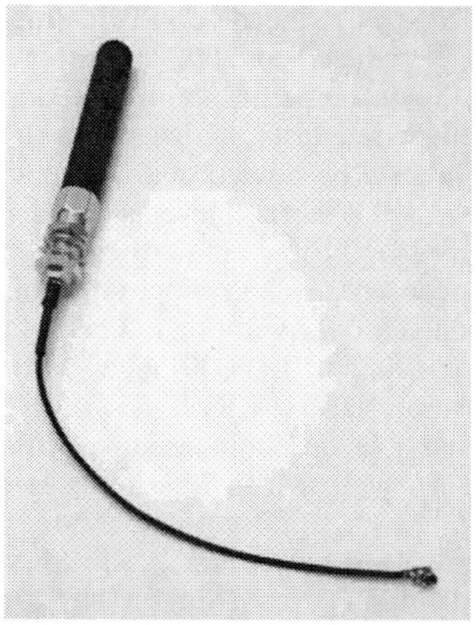

Figure 4. 868 MHz antenna.

The tests were performed on a wide street with buildings on one side and fields on the other side (see Figure 5). The satellite image of the area where the measures were taken is provided in Figure 6, with the street highlighted in yellow. The emitter was placed at the beginning of the street and the receiver moved to different measuring points.

Figure 5. Location of the tests.

Figure 6. Satellite image of the location of the tests.

There were no obstructions between the emitter and receiver nodes. The RSSI was obtained for each of the measuring points. Moreover, the test was repeated for each of the antennas and each of the SF for the corresponding frequency band.

## IV. Results

In this section, the results from the performed tests are presented.

The results for the 868 MHz frequency band with the 3 dBi antenna are presented in Figure 7. As it can be seen, the RSSI values presented fluctuations for all the SF even in the absence of obstacles. The SF 7 was the one with the better signal at close distances. However, as the distance increased, other SF configurations presented better results. On the other hand, the SF 11 was the one with the overall worst RSSI values. The rest of the SF configurations have obtained similar RSSI values. Therefore, for this frequency band and this type of antenna, the selection of the SF does not seem to have a significant impact o the quality of the signal. So, other aspects should be considered for the selection of the best SF.

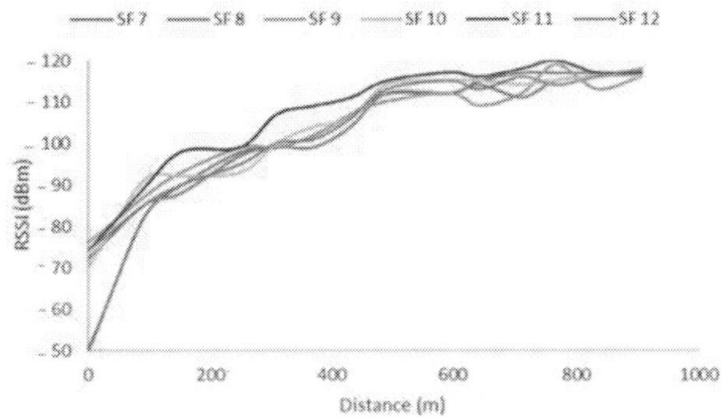


Figure 7. RSSI for 868 MHz and 3dBi antenna.

The results for the 433 MHz frequency band and the 3dBi antenna are shown in Figure 8. In this case, it is more evident that the SF 7 configuration leads to better signal quality. Although for the last measuring point, the RSSI values of SF 7 are similar to those of the rest of the SF configurations. The SF 10 is the second-best configuration, with the other SF configurations having lower signal quality. Moreover, SF 11 would be the SF with the worst RSSI values. As the difference between SF configurations is more evident for this antenna, the selection of the SF should be considered when designing a LoRa network with these devices. However, it would apply mostly for the SF 7 configuration, as the other SF present fewer differences.

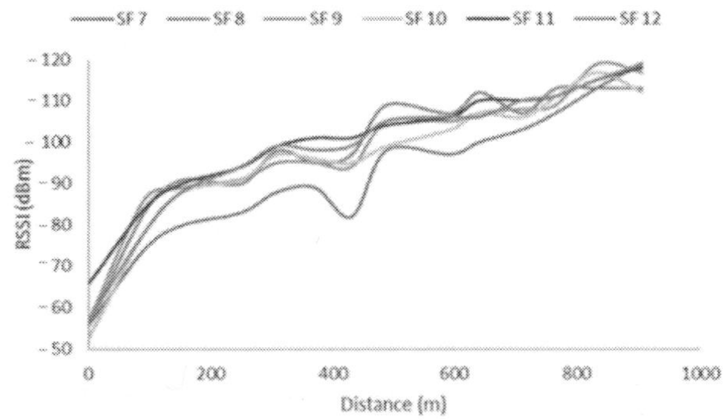


Figure 8. RSSI for 433 MHz and 3dBi antenna.

Lastly, Figure 9 shows the RSSI values for the frequency band of 433 MHz and the antenna of 5 dBi. SF 7 and SF 10 have the best signal quality. However, there is not a clear difference between SF configurations as in the case of Figure 8. On the other hand, SF 11 and 12 present the worst signal quality, with little difference between both configurations. The rest of the SF configurations present similar results to those of SF7 ad SF 10. As in the case of the 868 MHz frequency band, there is no highly noticeable difference between the different SF values, therefore, other aspects should be considered when selecting the best configuration.

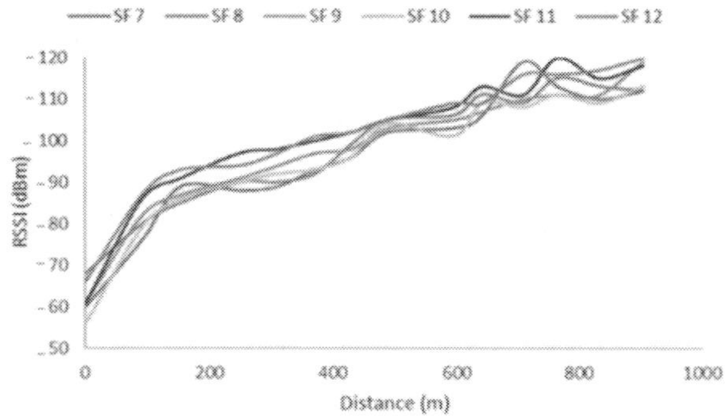


Figure 9. RSSI for 433 MHz and 5dBi antenna.

Figure 10 presents the average values of all SF values for each frequency band and antenna in order to compare the three studied cases. As it can be seen, on average, the two antennas for the 433 MHz frequency band have similar results. However, the average shows better results for the 3 dBi antenna due to the less noticeable difference between the results for each SF. Regarding the 868 MHz frequency band, the average of the RSSI values shows a lower image quality than that of transmitting with 433 MHz.

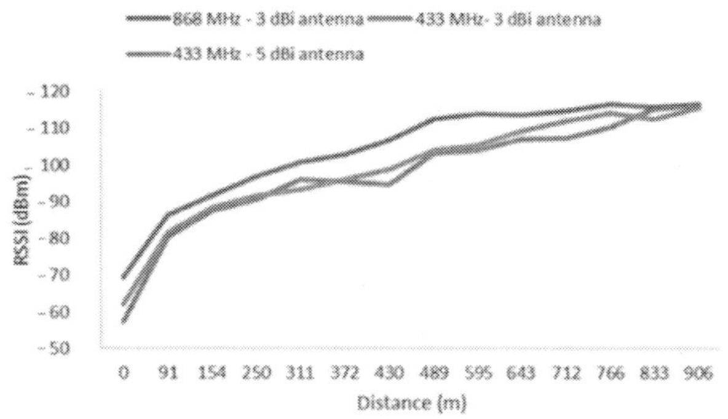


Figure 10. Average RSSI for each frequency band and antenna.

Considering the results for all the cases, we can conclude that the use of low-cost LoRa devices and antennas cannot be advised for distance requirements larger than 1 km. In those cases, other solutions such as multi-hop LoRa protocols should be employed to transmit the data to the desired location. Furthermore, the difference in the gain of the antennas for the 433 MHz frequency band was not reflected in the obtained results. For the case of the 868 MHz frequency band, the difference in SF configurations barely affects the received quality of the signal.

## V. Conclusion and Future Work

As LoRa gains more interest, the deployment of LoRa devices in locations such as cities, fields, or sensor buoys. LoRa transmissions have reached record distances up to 832 km. Moreover, although the expected distances range from 10 to 40 km depending on the obstructions in the area, low-cost LoRa devices do not reach those expectations. In this paper, we have performed coverage tests with cost-effective LoRa devices and antennas. The RSSI was measured for the frequency bands of 433 MHz and 868 MHz, all the SF configurations, and antennas with gains of 3 dBi and 5 dBi in line-of-sight conditions. The results show that the selection of different SF may not affect the quality of the received signal, such as for the 868 MHz frequency band. Furthermore, the combination of low-cost LoRa devices and low-cost antennas does not provide coverage greater than 1 km. Therefore, other solutions, such as multi-hop LoRa networks should be implemented when there is an interest in deploying low-cost devices.

For future work, we will perform tests with LoRa devices and antennas in the medium price range. Furthermore, tests will be performed with different types of content, such as data from sensors or images so as to assess the performance of LoRa and the devices with different traffic demands. Lastly, a multi-hop solution will be created to increase the distance achieved by LoRa networks.

## Acknowledgment

This work has been partially funded by the European Union through the ERANETMED (Euromediterranean Cooperation through ERANET joint activities and beyond) project ERANETMED3-227 SMARTWATIR, by the the "Programa Estatal de I+D+i Orientada a los Retos de la Sociedad, en el marco del Plan Estatal de Investigación Científica y Técnica y de Innovación 2017-2020" (Project code: PID2020-114467RR-C33) and by "proyectos de innovación de interés general por grupos operativos de la Asociación Europea para la Innovación en materia de productividad y sostenibilidad agrícolas (AEI-Agri)" in the framework "Programa Nacional de Desarrollo Rural 2014-2020", GO TECNOGAR. This work has also been partially funded by the Universitat Politècnica de València through the post-doctoral PAID-10-20 program.

## References

[1] What are LoRa and LoRaWAN?, LoRa Developer Portal. [Online]. Available from: https://lora-developers.semtech.com/library/tech-papers-and-guides/lora-and-lorawan/ [Retrieved: June, 2021].

[2] Specifications LoRaWAN. [Online]. Available from: https://lora-alliance.org/resource_hub/what-is-lorawan/ [Retrieved: June, 2021]

[3] J. M. Jimenez, et al. "New Protocol and Architecture for a Wastewater Treatment System intended for Irrigation", Applied Sciences, vol. 11, No. 8, pp. 3648, 2021.

[4] S. Sendra, L. García, J. Lloret, I. Bosch, and R. Vega-Rodríguez, "LoRaWAN network for fire monitoring in rural environments", Electronics, vol. 9, No. 3, pp. 531, 2020.

[5] A. Abrado, and A. Pozzebon, "A Multi-Hop LoRa Linear Sensor Network for the Monitoring of Underground Environments: The Case of the Medieval Aqueducts in Siena, Italy", Sensors, vol. 19, pp. 402, 2019.

[6] L. Xia, Z. Jiandao, and W. Huafeng, "A LoRa Buoy Network Coverage Optimization Algorithm Based on Virtual Force", 2nd IEEE International Conference on Information Communication and Signal Processing, Weihai, China, 28-30 September 2019, pp. 204-209.

[7] LoRa World Record Broken: 832km/517mi using 25mW, The things Network. [Online]. Available from: https://www.thethingsnetwork.org/article/lorawan-world-record-broken-twice-in-single-experiment-1 [Retrieved: June, 2021]

[8] F. J. Grión, G. O. Petracca, D. F. Lipuma, and E. R. Amigó, "LoRa Network Coverage Evaluation in Urban and Densely Urban Environment: Simulation and validation tests in Autonomous City of Buenos Aires", XVII Workshop on Information Processing and Control (RPIC), Mar del Plata, Argentina, 20-22 September 2017, pp. 1-5.

[9] J. C. Liando, A. Gamage, A. W. Tengourtius, and M. Li, "Known and Unknown Facts of LoRa: Experiences from a Large-scale Measurement Study", ACM Transactions on Sensor Networks, vol. 15, No. 2, pp. 1-35, 2019.

[10] M. R. Seye, B. Gueye, and M. Diallo, "An Evaluation of LoRa Coverage in Dakar Peninsula", 8th IEEE Annual Information Technology, Electronics and Mobile Communication Conference, Vancouver, Canada, 3-5 October 2017, pp. 478-482.

[11] M. R. Seye, B. Ngom, B. Gueye, and M. Diallo, "A Study of LoRa Coverage: Range Evaluation and Channel Attenuation Model", 1st International Conference on Smart Cities and Communities (SCCIC), Ouagadougou, Burkina Faso, 24-26 July 2018, pp. 1-4.

[12] M. Lauridsen, et al. "Coverage comparison of GPRS, NB-IoT, LoRa, and SigFox in 7800 km2 area", IEEE 85th Vehicular Technology Conference, Sydney, Australia, 4-7 June 2017, pp. 1-5.

[13] B. Vejlgaard, et al. "Coverage and Capacity Analysis of Sigfox, LoRa, GPRS and NB-IoT", IEEE 85th Vehicular Technology Conference, Sydney, Australia, 4-7 June 2017, pp. 1-5.

[14] G. Zhu, C. Liao, M. Suzuki, Y. Narusue, and H. Morikawa, "Evaluation of LoRa Receiver Performance under Co-technology Interference.", 15th IEEE Annual Consumer Communications & Networking Conference, Las Vegas, USA, 12-15 January 2018, pp. 1-7.

[15] M. Marchese, A. Moheddine, and F. Patrone, "Towards Increasing the LoRa Network Coverage: A Flying Gateway", International Symposium on Advanced Electrical and Communication Technologies, Rome, Italy, 27-29 November 2019, pp. 1-4.

[16] Heltec WiFi LoRa 32 (v2). [Online]. Available from: https://heltec.org/project/wifi-lora-32/ [Retrieved: June, 2021]